LIFE MOMENTS WITH JOY

JOY BACH

WORDS BY DESIGN

Life Moments with Joy
Published by Words by Design
www.joy-lifemoments.blogspot.com

© 2017 Joy Bach

ISBN: 978-0-9994956-0-5 (paperback)

Cover Design: Matt McClay, McClay Design
Layout & Editing: Deborah Porter, Finesse Writing & Editing Service

Lovingly Dedicated to My Husband

When the word "cancer" entered our world, it began to destroy John's body, but could not touch his spirit. His desire was that his cancer journey not be wasted; that others would see Jesus shining through. He gave his treatment and outcome to God.

Today, John's words of encouragement wrap me in love. I can still hear him say, "I know you can do it," when we discussed the publication of this book.

Introduction

GREETINGS, ALL. I'M HERE to say a few words about Joy Bach.

Joy is real, and she seems to have somehow inherited the art of relating her own life experiences in a way that not only tells her story, but also brings reality and conclusion, including how she's managed to come through, and go forward, one step at a time.

Some would say "inspirational."

Others might say Joy is "strong."

I say she's "realistic."

Yes, Joy is real, and her "stories" are non-fiction. Many have discovered her ability to reach out from dark places with light.

And yes, I do have a quite realistic awareness of her life. I've known her for a very long time. Joy is my baby sister.

Carl Vail
October, 2017

Contents

Your joy will be a river overflowing its banks!
John 16:24

Messing With My Mind

WHEN I LEAVE HOME for the gym at five in the morning, bleary-eyed and half awake, I have to work hard to remember what I need to take with me—my car keys, sheet of paper with the routines I do, water, iPhone to listen to a podcast, headphones to be able to do that, and the key to get into the gym.

One morning, I was sure I had remembered everything. When I go through the routines, I place most of my items in a cubby provided by the gym. After I'm through with the machines, I'm ready for my water and headphones as I walk on the treadmill. I had my iPhone in my pocket, but when I reached for the water bottle, it was not there. In my mind's eye, I could see me pick up the water bottle at home and take it to the car. *Guess I left it in the car.*

After a trip to the car, I was still waterless. So for the next thirty minutes, I walked and listened, but did not drink. When I went to the cubby to get my other stuff, there sat my water bottle, still full of water.

Where did that come from? Who took it? Is it safe to drink now?

Whether on purpose or by accident, someone definitely messed with my mind that morning.

Life is like that. We do everything humanly possible to get our stuff together. We have our routines, a time slot for this and another slot for that. Occasionally, something isn't in the right spot. The out-of-place thing may be something tangible, like losing your car keys. Other times, it's an emotional piece that may go missing. Maybe someone turned on you and said hurtful things. *Where did that come from?* you wonder. Maybe a loved one took advantage of you in the past and now they are back in your life. *Are they safe to trust now or will they just use me again?*

Life messes with our minds.

I chose to drink the water . . . and I turn to God to help me deal with the other stuff.

Psalm 9:9-10

"God's a safe-house for the battered, a sanctuary during bad times. The moment you arrive, you relax; you're never sorry you knocked."

The Source

I LISTENED INTENTLY TO Chuck Swindoll as I worked steadily to prune my garden. Suddenly, Chuck went silent. I had cut the cord to my headphones.

Another day, as I vacuumed my way across the room, I felt the cord hold me back, so I gave a little tug. No more suction. I'd pulled the plug from the power outlet in the wall.

I have an atomic clock, which operates on a signal sent from Colorado. One day, after moving a metal file cabinet into my office, I noticed the clock no longer kept perfect time. After moving the clock to several different locations, I realized the file cabinet had blocked the signal.

In each of these incidents, I was no longer connected to the source. Chuck was still speaking, but I no longer received his message. The electricity did not suddenly disappear from my home, but there was no connection to the vacuum cleaner. That signal from Colorado still beamed out across the airwaves, but my clock couldn't receive the information. I'd allowed something to get in the way.

As a Christ-follower, I have a Source that is steadfast and eternal. His message is always there, His power never goes off, and He constantly sends His love and care across the airwaves. It's up to me to ensure nothing cuts off or blocks my connection.

In the same way my carelessness caused the cord to be cut, I can become thoughtless and unconcerned in my walk with Christ. If I'm not observant of my own actions, I can become unplugged from my power Source, leaving me depressed and empty. And there are many ways to block His signal from entering my life. When I allow these impediments, I stray off course and become an ineffective witness to God's love and compassion.

Isaiah 40:29-31

"He doesn't get tired out, doesn't pause to catch his breath. And he knows everything, inside and out. He energizes those who get tired, gives fresh strength to dropouts. For even young people tire and drop out, young folk in their prime stumble and fall. But those who wait upon God get fresh strength. They spread their wings and soar like eagles, they run and don't get tired, they walk and don't lag behind."

Light in the Laundry Room

WE HAD A DEVICE installed on the light switch in the laundry room. It senses our presence when we walk into that room and turns on the light. Such a deal.

It took me time to get used to it, and my hand still reaches for the switch now and then.

But it started me thinking (and I can't seem to stop).

I can't stand in the kitchen and expect the laundry room light to come on.

In the same way, I have to choose to stay in God's presence in order to see His light. The further away from Him I move, the less likely I am to follow His light.

The world is full of temptations, but I'm staying in the laundry room.

Hebrews 10:19
"So, friends, we can now—without hesitation—walk right up to God . . ."

The Meeting

THE MEETING WAS TO start at 7:30, but we were requested to be there by 7:15 to get the paperwork out of the way before starting time. As I rounded the corner to the meeting room, I was surprised by the line of people snaking out the door and into the hallway. *This is going to be good!*

I signed in, received my folder and nametag, and headed for a seat. The leader stood in front of us, her smile lighting up the room. I looked around and realized I knew a lot of the people . . . even some of their families. My anticipation built. I'd been in meetings with this leader before. It was going to be a great night.

We opened in prayer and the atmosphere in the room began to change. The talking and hubbub settled down. We knew God was going to be with us as we worked our way through the folder.

Before we started the official meeting, I saw the words on the first page. Words about running to the Lord, no one else will do . . . about God being our ever-present help in time of trouble. I had been having some health issues, so these words were a balm to my spirit.

There were more words on more pages, and as those words made their way into our hearts, the air became electric. I felt the connection as we all concentrated on God and what He has done for us.

Some hands went into the air. One of them was mine. How could I not praise Him?

We were nearing the end of the folder and God's presence was so very real. I felt the need to stand in reverence. Soon everyone was standing.

We were at the end of our folder and our words. With a prayer of blessing on us, we were free to go home, renewed in our spirits.

Choir practice was over for another week.

Psalm 108:1-2

"I'm ready, God, so ready, ready from head to toe. Ready to sing, ready to raise a God-song: "Wake, soul! Wake, lute! Wake up, you sleepyhead sun!"

My Quest for Jeans

WEARING PANTS WAS A sin. That was a fact in my growing up world. I was in my 30s before I reconsidered that premise by looking at some dress slacks, and then actually purchasing and wearing them. But jeans? That would be a stretch.

Then I became friends with Linda, who seemed to live in denim. One day she asked why I never wore jeans. I had no good answer, and so began my quest to find some jeans I liked. I went shopping (which is one of my *least* favorite things to do).

Over the next few years, I'd try on a pair, think they would work, buy them, wear them a few times, and then they would hang in my closet. Finally, off they went to Goodwill, or maybe to a friend who could use them.

My quest continued.

Occasionally, Linda and I would return to the jeans conversation. She was delighted I was searching for a pair. Then the unthinkable happened. Linda was murdered. The quest for jeans was pushed aside.

Eventually, I began looking again and it seemed as though Linda was right beside me.

Then one day, when I needed to purchase something totally unrelated to jeans, I happened to walk by a display of jeans. Pausing, I recognized the brand. It was a brand I was comfortable in with other kinds of pants. What if these were the ones?

Not even bothering to try them on, I bought a pair and took them home. My husband John and I planned to attend a motorcycle rally that weekend, which involved camping out. My new jeans would be good to have.

And they fit.

I returned to the store and bought a second pair.

Sitting in the campground, wearing my jeans, I could see Linda smiling.

Matthew 6:28 (NASB)

"And why are you worried about clothing? Observe how the lilies of the field grow; they do not toil nor do they spin . . ."

Necco Therapy

I LISTENED TO THE river as it sang its song. The sound blotted out the world around me and I was alone with thoughts I didn't want.

Why?

Why had he called and said those words?

Why pick the scab off the healing sore?

Or was it festering underneath? The pain and bitterness flowing from within me was as though someone had lanced an infected wound.

I watched the swirling water forever flowing, breaking and spraying over the rocks. Listlessly, I ate Necco candy wafers, tossing the colors I didn't want into the rushing torrent. They disappeared from sight, and then bobbed up, flowing with the current around the large rock in the center and on to the ocean. Each one reacted differently.

My thoughts swirled in tune with the river.

I had been divorced three years. He had remarried, but I was still working at picking up the pieces and making a family from three daughters and myself.

And then he called.

Again my mind turned to the river.

The water crashed on the big boulder in the middle of the river, splashing into tiny particles of moisture. Then it fell back to the river, merged with the water, and continued its journey.

I watched a black wafer sink deeper and deeper with the undertow. It fought upwards. Leaping to the surface, it skimmed merrily along the top of the water.

My inner eyes began to see.

My life was like that river and I was a Necco wafer. My ex-husband was that big boulder in the middle, and I had been broken to a thousand pieces. Yet, it was not my task to remove the boulder. My duty was to go over, around, or under the immovable object and continue my journey.

My favorite part of the river was the rapids, with beauty in the foam and spray, and peaceful harmony in its loud, clear song.

Could this be true with life? Was it possible the beauty was in the rapids?

Time seemed to stand still.

My thoughts swirled, but I felt a release of pressure. The pungent sensation gave way to a refreshing awareness of life and its beauty. The knowledge that I would have other boulders in my river was no longer foreboding.

Peace flooded my inner being.
I had forgiven him.

Hebrews 12:15

"Keep a sharp eye out for weeds of bitter discontent. A thistle or two gone to seed can ruin a whole garden in no time."

My Little Black Box

IT WAS A UNIQUE experience when I became, temporarily, tethered to a fanny pack that was never to be more than three feet from my body. No matter what I was doing—whether exercising, showering, or sleeping—I was very aware of exactly where that little monitor was.

From deep inside my body, a signal transmitted information to the little black box. Later, when I returned the monitor to the doctor, a record of that information was printed out for the doctor to review.

As I kept track of the monitor's location, my mind turned to my Christian walk. Exactly how close do I keep Christ? Am I aware, every moment, of His proximity? Do I exercise, shower, and sleep with Him in mind?

And what about the signal I'm sending from deep within me? What kind of information am I transmitting? Do I really want those thoughts recorded and printed out for God to review some day?

Where's your fanny pack?

Matthew 6:16

"When you practice some appetite-denying discipline to better concen-trate on God, don't make a production out of it. It might turn you into a small-time celebrity but it won't make you a saint."

Life in a Saltshaker

THE PEWS WOULD BE full—Sunday morning and evening, Wednesday night prayer meeting, and every evening all week when it was revival time. The saints would gather, nodding at each other as they took their assigned seats. Some shouting would be heard, some fingers pointed, as the worshipers expressed their agreement with the words being spoken.

Then they all went home and waited for the next time to come together.

When the boundaries of the church property were reached, the armor was in place so no dirt from the world could possibly affect them.

As they traveled through their days, no eye contact was made with the heathen outside the church. *What a pity they don't come into the fold and be saved,* the pious ones would think.

The problem was that those churchgoers never left the saltshaker. Nothing was made better by them because they didn't desire to be sprinkled in the world.

Even as I lived in this secluded world, it didn't seem right. Yet I carried on the tradition of exclusivity until I was in my 30s. When I studied the Bible for myself, instead of being told what to believe, I came across a scripture that made my heart say *ah ha*.

Matthew 5:13

"Let me tell you why you are here. You're here to be salt-seasoning that brings out the God-flavors of this earth. If you lose your saltiness, how will people taste godliness? You've lost your usefulness and will end up in the garbage."

That sounds to me like we're supposed to do more than just go to church. As a Christ-follower, I'm supposed to be good for the world. I can't do that if I live my life in the saltshaker.

I still go to church. It's a gathering of my friends, but doing church is no longer my focus. These days, I rub elbows with people who occasionally use the f-word. I don't like it . . . and they know it. They've gotten to know me, and what I stand for, and now they apologize when they slip up.

That's an opening for me to sprinkle a little salt.

Have you ever over-salted something? Then you know it destroys the enjoyment of eating that food. Just a little salt, when needed, does the job.

My Keycard

THE GYM WHERE I exercise is called Club 24. The name explains it. You can go there any time—day or night—and gain entrance with your keycard.

The other morning I dressed for exercise, then drove to the gym. I parked the car, grabbed my water bottle, headphones, iPhone, and keycard, and walked to the front door. I pulled on the door handle and it didn't open. *What's up?*

Duh. I hadn't swiped my keycard.

Once I did that, the door opened freely.

Being a Christian is like that. Christ is available any time—day or night.

You may dress for church, carry your Bible, and listen to sermons, but unless you have a relationship with Christ, the door will remain shut and you'll be left standing on the outside looking in.

Matthew 7:21a

"Not everyone who says to Me, 'Lord, Lord,' will enter the kingdom of heaven . . ."

Under Construction

ONE YEAR. WE HAD been in our wonderful new home for one year.

As I walked through the rooms, I remembered watching the house go up. First it was just a hole in the ground. Next came the huge concrete slab.

Every day, John and I would drive to the construction site and view the progress. Some days it looked the same as the day before. Other days the house had suddenly taken on a different personality.

We would step through the uncompleted rooms, discussing how it would be when a wall was in place. At the time, it was hard to visualize the finished product.

One day, a huge piece of equipment arrived. It was time to pour the outside walls. The concrete mixer turned around and around as the liquid concrete moved through a chute to travel way high in the air, far higher than the light poles. It took two men on the ground to guide the hose full of concrete to the correct spot to fill.

Windows.

Tile.

Roof.

A wonderful new home was being created before us.

As human beings, we are also under construction. Sometimes the progress isn't visible to anyone else. Other times, everyone can notice the change. From the moment of our conception, we have been growing and changing. God designed it that way. We are exactly as He planned in His blueprint.

How's your house coming along?

Psalm 139:15

"You know me inside and out, you know every bone in my body; you know exactly how I was made, bit by bit, how I was sculpted from nothing into something."

Spaghetti

THE SUPERSHUTTLE VAN FLEW down the freeway headed for LAX. John and I had been on a trip to the Los Angeles area and now it was time to return home.

Everywhere I looked, through the shuttle window, I could see cars hurrying somewhere. The exit ramps flew by, and sometimes the interchanges were three levels deep. It reminded me of spaghetti.

A few cars would brake slightly as they approached an exit. Maybe they weren't sure it was the right one, or maybe they were afraid to merge with the next highway.

Some vehicles rounded the exit ramp so quickly I feared they would turn over. They were on a mission.

Then there was the constant merging of cars. It was a veritable sea of movement in every direction. The result of one wrong move would be an accident.

The shuttle driver's window was down and the noise was overwhelming. Suddenly, I heard a thud. I looked out my window in time to see a car scrape down the concrete divider that separated them from us.

Thoughts flitted through my mind.

What would have happened if that divider had not been there?

Was the car disabled?

Was anyone hurt?

There was no way to know as we continued our mad dash to the airport.

My thoughts turned to life—specifically, my life. I understood that hesitancy when approaching exit ramps. I had uprooted my children and moved us to a different state, but what if it was the wrong exit? How far would I have to travel before I knew I'd made a mistake? Could I ever get back?

I've faced so many different exits in my life, so much spaghetti. Each exit was a new and different decision, but making decisions wasn't easy for me, and certainly not at the speed my new life required. Most people were in a hurry with their own lives and wanted me to move to the right and let them pass.

Ever been there?

God is ever ready with the directions for you, but you have to listen to hear them.

Are you so sure of your direction that you don't even bother asking if you're going the right way? Where has that led you so far?

Remove yourself from the spaghetti and slow down enough to see the signs along the way. Read the Bible. Talk with a pastor.

God loves you and wants the best for you. If you've taken a wrong exit, He is waiting to help.

Psalm 23:3

"True to your word, you let me catch my breath and send me in the right direction".

Yard Work

DURING THE FIRST YEAR in our new home we spent a lot of time taking care of the sod, trying to give it a good start. Then came winter.

The next spring, we discovered an accumulation of tumbleweeds and other debris that had built up behind the garage and against the gate. We removed the trash, but the sod in that area did not recover. We had to replace it.

Most of our lawn was nice and green, except for a few small spots where the grass struggled. And then there was that one larger area that needed a little more tender loving care. We kept an eye on its progress.

Life is like that. We have people in our lives that are easy to be around. They don't take much work and they provide pleasure. Others are a little more high maintenance. With those people, we need to be careful about certain topics, and sometimes they're in a bad mood. And what about that one person who always seems to need all the attention?

Then there are people like that one corner in our yard. They have so many traumas in their life that they can't seem to recover. We have a choice with those people. We can let them slowly die away, or we can bring in some new sod and try to be a catalyst for them to thrive.

My relationship lawn resembles my physical one.

How does your lawn look?

Colossians 3:12

"So, chosen by God for this new life of love, dress in the wardrobe God picked out for you: compassion, kindness, humility, quiet strength, discipline . . ."

On My Horizon

THE VIEW FROM MY neighborhood is the steam cloud rising from the Hanford Nuclear Site. It is a constant on my horizon, but following the tragedy and subsequent ramifications of the Fukashima nuclear disaster in Japan, the cloud is a daily reminder of the possible danger in my own area of the country.

But what about other dangers that can be on anyone's horizon?

How about health dangers? America has become a nation of obese people. The Internet, newspapers, magazines, and television all report the statistics on the dangers of obesity. In the same way that steam cloud looms on my horizon, a stroke or heart attack may loom in the distance of my health. I have struggled with overeating my whole life and I understand how hard it is to control. Do I really see that health issue on my horizon? Do you?

What about living with an abusive spouse? Again, the media is full of statistics about the maiming and death of people at the hands of their "loved" ones. Do you see signals that your life is in danger? Or have you placed your head in the sand, believing it could never happen to you?

The list could go on and on.

You know if you have a possible danger on your horizon.

Please don't learn to live with it.

Matthew 10:29-31 (NLT)

"What is the price of two sparrows—one copper coin? But not a single sparrow can fall to the ground without your Father knowing it. And the very hairs on your head are all numbered. So don't be afraid; you are more valuable to God than a whole flock of sparrows."

Pattern Choices

BORED WITH CROCHETING AFTER years of the craft, I attended a knitting class where we were given a choice of beginner patterns to try. Each week, the teacher helped me understand the pattern I had chosen and the stitch I needed to use to achieve the desired result. The completed vest became a gift for one of my daughters.

After knitting for a while, I began to intersperse my projects with crocheting, but no matter the type of project, they had one thing in common—I made mistakes. Sometimes I could fix the mistake, but a few times I had to unravel and start over.

In one of my knitting projects, I had worked for months on an afghan for a daughter. I was using circular needles, which are one long plastic strand with a needle point on each end. As my needle went in and out, the tension on it suddenly lessened. Not sure what had happened, I laid the partially finished afghan on the floor. In horror, I saw that one of the needle points had come off the plastic strand. I had several inches of knitted loops with nothing holding them in place. My project was ruined.

I didn't know how to fix it, but I remembered the name of my knitting teacher. Hurrying to the phone book, I found her telephone number. When she answered the phone, I poured my distress out to her.

She came right over, bringing a new circular needle for me to borrow. With expertise, she methodically picked through the loops and restored my afghan. When finished with the rescue, she refused to take any form of payment, telling me she was glad to help.

The Bible contains many different types of patterns. There are designs for Christian living, relationships, and parenting, to name a few. In Ephesians 5:21-33, there is a pattern for marriage.

God has given us various colored threads to use. Sometimes it will be tedious and require a lot of give and take. We will have tangled threads and dropped loops, and it will be a long time before we begin to see the finished design.

There will also be times when we don't quite understand the project we've chosen and need help from our Teacher.

In our distress, we can turn to the One who already knows how the finished project should look. He has the expertise to repair our design. If we allow Him, He will pick through our dropped stitches and restore us to wholeness.

1 Peter 5:10

"It won't be long before this generous God who has great plans for us in Christ—eternal and glorious plans they are!—will have you put together and on your feet for good."

In Sync

When I purchased an iPhone, I had to learn a lot of new technical words, including *sync*. I was told my phone would need to be synced on a regular basis. I was clueless. But I learned.

My iPhone came with accessories. One was a cord with plugs on each end. This was to be used for syncing. One end plugged into my iPhone, the other end into my computer. And then they talked to each other. This kept my phone updated.

One day, I made the magic connection between my computer and iPhone, and within seconds, it showed the sync was complete. I had my doubts, but unplugged the phone and hurried on my way.

This scenario was repeated the next few times I synced. Then I began to notice that information was not being transferred between the devices. There was a malfunction in my sync. I had to turn to Apple Care for answers.

Some time after, there was a special service at my church. Since I was in the choir, I was at the church for both services.

At the first service, the pastor spoke of the Old Testament and God's way of using prophets to speak for him to mankind. As the sermon continued, the pastor explained that the priests were used to speak to God for mankind. He concluded his message by saying that, today, Jesus does both.

I climbed the steps to the risers to join the choir in singing the last song, but my mind was still on the sermon. I felt like I had missed something important, so I sat through the second service.

When the message began, I started looking for a pencil and paper so I could take notes. That's when I remembered I could take notes on my iPhone. Duh!

As the pastor repeated his thoughts about prophets, priests, and now Jesus, it all clicked.

Jesus is the one who keeps us in sync. If we stay plugged in, we will be in constant contact with the source of our program. We can talk to Him and know that He listens. Upgrades are available when we plug into the Bible, sermons, Christian music, and alone time with Him.

Jesus is *far* better than Apple Care.

It was a timely message for me. I knew I was out of sync, so I put in an emergency call to my Service Provider. He hadn't taken the evening off, and I was soon back in sync.

Isaiah 58:9 (NLT)

"Then when you call, the Lord will answer. 'Yes, I am here,' He will quickly reply."

And So I Ponder

HE SAT ON THE sidewalk, leaning against the traffic light pole. I walked within touching distance and could easily read his sign: "I have colon cancer and am taking chemo. Have lost my job. Can you help?"

We made eye contact. I didn't mean to. That made it all the harder to step down from the curb and walk across the street, not looking back. My heart was heavy. What kind of a Christian am I?

And they were everywhere in Seattle: men and women, skinny as rails, dirty with ragged clothes. Some had a dog by their side, which made me wonder why, if they were starving, would they have a dog to feed? But what if that dog was their only companionship? How is it my place to judge?

I spent several days in Seattle, enjoying my husband's company, staying in a nice hotel, eating in the restaurants of our choice, and having a wonderful time. Still, those people nagged in the back of my mind.

I've heard the stories. For some, this is how they earn their living. At the end of the day, they go home to a real house with a real family. They are the fake homeless, but how do we know which are the real?

Others, sadly, have mental issues. I want to put them in my car and take them home.

In circumstances like this, how do we know what to do?

I have felt this way before. That's the reason I never want to go to Mexico again, with little children begging at my feet. They haunted me for months. I want millions of dollars and then I can fix it. Or can I?

Even though it is hard to believe, this is the life some have chosen. They have no bills and no boss to please. But then there are those who didn't plan this way of life. They've lost their job, their home, and their family. Those people are the true tragedies. They want to pay their own way, but feel humiliated by the life they lead.

And so I ponder.

Luke 6:31

"Ask . . . what you want people to do for you; then grab the initiative and do it for *them*!"

Let's Have a Party Before We Die

MORRIE SCHWARTZ HAD A choice. In his book, *Tuesdays with Morrie*, he asks, "Do I wither up and disappear, or do I make the best of my time left?"

His doctors told him he had two years, but he knew he was living the last year of his life. So Morrie had what he called a "living funeral." He got to hear all the wonderful things his friends would have said after he died. Morrie laughed and cried with them. His "living funeral" was a success.

As I read that book, I thought about the way we (in America) view dying. Many people feel uncomfortable and avoid the dying one, but they spiff up their clothes and shine their shoes to attend the funeral. I guess they feel safe then.

Why don't we tell people all the wonderful things we think about them while they are still alive to hear it?

If you knew your time on this earth was limited, would you have a party? Jesus did. His time was limited, yet He spent the last hours of His life eating dinner with His closest friends. He knew the torture and horrible death He was about to face, but He took time to sit and visit with His disciples, communicating His last important words to them.

We are all in the process of dying. Of course, we know that in our head, but do we really believe it in our heart? If we did, wouldn't we be more involved in life now, reaching out to others? The death of a loved one makes us sad, but how grievous it is to live an empty life of chasing a bigger paycheck instead of learning to love and be loved in return.

Once we learn how to die, then we will have learned how to live.

Mark 14:13-16 (NLT)

"So Jesus sent two of them into Jerusalem with these instructions: "As you go into the city, a man carrying a pitcher of water will meet you. Follow him. At the house he enters, say to the owner, 'The Teacher asks: Where is the guest room where I can eat the Passover meal with my disciples?' He will take you upstairs to a large room that is already set up. That is where you should prepare our meal." So the two disciples went into the city and found everything just as Jesus had said, and they prepared the Passover meal there."

Oh What a Day

In the wee hours of the morning—1:00 AM to be exact—on April 29, 2011, the television coverage of the royal wedding of Prince William and Catherine Middleton began. Some folks in our time zone didn't bother going to bed, but I did. I figured I could watch any highlights later.

People in London camped out for several days along the procession route, so they could catch a glimpse of history in the making.

In Florida, another kind of history was scheduled . . . the launch of the final flight of the space shuttle *Endeavour* with Commander Mark Kelly in charge of the six-man crew.

I find it ironic that we know Commander Kelly as the husband of Rep. Gabrielle Giffords, who had been shot during a constituent meeting in January that year. Three months later, she had been allowed to leave her rehab in Houston to travel to Florida for her husband's launch. The news reports gave us our first picture of her since the shooting as she climbed the steps to the airplane.

An estimated crowd of 700,000 gathered at the launch site to mark one more thing off their bucket list, but the van carrying the crew to the launch platform made a U-turn, never completing the trip. The launch was postponed.

April 29, 2011, would have been Dale Earnhardt's 60th birthday. He lost his life in 2001 on the last lap of the Daytona 500.

I discovered Dale about the same time as I was crawling out of the pile of "shoulds, oughts, and have tos" I had grown up with. As I watched Dale fearlessly drive 190 MPH, aiming his car for a hole that was not yet there, he helped teach me about life.

There were those who didn't like Dale, and it didn't bother him a bit. What a lesson. Until then, I had lived my life trying to please *everyone*.

Racing is not the same without him.

Also on this day, in an operating room in Seattle, a friend of mine underwent an eight-hour cranial surgery to remove a tumor.

The newspaper that morning stated that 297 people were killed by tornadoes that twisted their way across the south. Families had been allowed to return to where their homes once stood, to dig through the rubble and look for mementoes of a life that is gone.

On this most eventful day, I felt blessed beyond measure. I could see, walk, hear, eat, laugh, and love. My home was in one piece. I was able to pay bills and have some money left. My husband came home from work and we spent some time together.

Life is like that. The good and the bad . . . all in one day.

Romans 8:39

"I'm absolutely convinced that nothing—nothing living or dead, angelic or demonic, today or tomorrow, high or low, thinkable or unthinkable— absolutely nothing can get between us and God's love because of the way that Jesus our Master has embraced us."

Ringing Doorbell

AFTER HAVING WORKED IN the yard, a hot shower was refreshing and cleansing. I had just rubbed the shampoo into my hair when the doorbell rang.

Oh great, I thought. *Well, they will have to wait.*

Then it occurred to me, *That didn't sound like our doorbell.*

Days before, I had set an alarm on my iPhone for something I would otherwise forget. I had chosen a doorbell ringtone. Now that reminder was ringing on and on.

Maybe it will stop after a minute.

But no, the doorbell continued to ring.

What an intrusion to my usual meditating and quiet time. How long would it go on?

As the ringing sounded throughout my bathroom, my thoughts turned to people in my life—people who are like that intrusive, continually ringing doorbell.

At least I could eventually turn the alarm off . . . even if I had to use a hammer.

People don't have an off button.

Romans 2:3-4

"You didn't think, did you, that just by pointing your finger at others you would distract God from seeing all your misdoings and from coming down on you hard? Or did you think that because he's such a nice God, he'd let you off the hook? Better think this one through from the beginning. God is kind, but he's not soft. In kindness he takes us firmly by the hand and leads us into a radical life-change."

Turning on the Light

THE LIGHT SWITCH SENSOR in our laundry room is a little sensitive. Even if I walk near the doorway, the light comes on. If it senses no more motion, it goes off.

One Friday night, we had a small gathering in our home to celebrate the first anniversary of living in our new home. On one of my trips to the kitchen to get something, I watched a hilarious routine unfold.

A friend was standing in the kitchen by the laundry room doorway, talking intently with someone. Occasionally, he would make some movement and the laundry room light would come on. With no break in the conversation, his hand would reach into the laundry room to turn the light off. Another movement from him and the light was back on.

He never took a break in his conversation to stop and check out the light switch and understand what was happening. Instead, he repeatedly tried to turn off the light.

I continued with my hostess duties and left him to fight the light battle on his own, but it got me thinking. That light *refused* to stay off when someone was near.

My Bible tells me I'm supposed to be a light in the darkness. Do I operate as well as the light in my laundry room? If I sense someone nearby, does my light come on? If they leave and come back repeatedly, do I finally give up and refuse to turn on again? Or can I be counted on to always give light when someone is close by?

Matthew 5:14

"Here's another way to put it: You're here to be light, bringing out the God-colors in the world. God is not a secret to be kept."

Pulling on the Leash

As soon as I reached for the leash, our dog, Charlie, would do a little dance. *Oh, boy, we're going on a walk.* Until we got a lead leash, he would near jerk my arm out of the socket with his pulling and running, always in a hurry to get to the next smell.

Charlie doesn't care much for the lead leash. It has a loop that goes around his snout, so when he pulls on the leash, his snout is pulled down. After a few times of that, he was willing to walk beside us.

I've observed his behavior and been reminded of how we live life. We are always pulling on the leash, wanting to run ahead to the next great thing. That might mean a new house, car, job, or spouse. The thought of walking patiently through life, perhaps actually planning for the financial needs ahead, pulls our snout down and we don't like it.

Whether Charlie pulls on the leash or not, the next bush, tree, pole, or fire hydrant will always be there for him. In the same way, our dreams and aspirations are waiting for us as we travel this journey.

If we could learn to enjoy the expectant feeling of what's ahead, the walk through life would be a lot more pleasant.

Luke 12:15

"Speaking to the people, he went on, "Take care! Protect yourself against the least bit of greed. Life is not defined by what you have, even when you have a lot.""

Touching Lives

EVERYONE SHE COMES IN contact with is touched by her life.

Members of her family have told me about the things she does that have affected their lives. I've heard stories from co-workers about what it was like to work with her. Former customers relate how it felt to be waited on by her.

And she touched my life.

After being around her, I would feel like pulling my hair out.

She was constantly discovering some new disease in her body. The weather was too hot . . . or too cold . . . or too sunny . . . or too cloudy. No matter how the conversation started, she always switched it to be about her.

She continues to touch lives.

We all touch other people's lives, and that can be a good or bad thing. It all depends on our attitude.

What kind of touching am I doing?

How about you?

James 4:1

"Where do you think all these appalling wars and quarrels come from? Do you think they just happen? Think again. They come about because you want your own way, and fight for it deep inside yourselves."

Next Time, I'm Taking a Jacket

It was cold . . . and I could see no indication that I would soon be warmer. The room was colder than outside, and I was attending an all-day meeting in it.

I glanced around at the other attendees and spied a man wearing a jacket. *Aha!* As the meeting began, I kept my eye on that jacket. When he took it off and hung it on the back of his chair, I saw my chance.

"Tom, would you mind if I borrowed your jacket? It is so cold in here and I didn't bring one."

Gentleman that he was, he promptly removed it from the chair and held it for me to put on. I snuggled into it and returned to my seat.

During the first break, I saw Tom heading toward me. *Oh no, he's coming to get his jacket.*

Not so. He needed to retrieve something from one of the pockets.

Within an hour, he was headed my way again. This time he needed something out of a different pocket.

As the day progressed, on a regular basis, Tom needed something from his jacket. It was like a comedy routine.

Then I realized that a lack of preparedness on my part had caused Tom to have a problem.

Isn't that what life is like? We don't plan our money wisely and suddenly there is too much outgo for the income. We don't prepare healthy food, so when we are hungry we eat badly.

Many times, when we have failed to plan, we turn to someone else for help. Does it matter to us that we have now caused a problem for them?

Tom never complained about the needed trips to his jacket. Other people we have used may not complain either. But how do they see us?

Next time, I'm taking a jacket.

Proverbs 22:7 (NASB)

"The rich rules over the poor, and the borrower becomes the lender's slave."

Simplifying

JOHN SAT BESIDE ME on the couch while objects kept flying by his head. Finally, he turned to me and asked, "What are you doing?"

"I'm simplifying".

I have a plan. I gather a pile of papers, magazines, or other stuff, then place the pile in my lap and simplify. Whatever is no longer necessary in my life, I fling toward the back door. The "keepables" are placed in proper stacks on the floor so they can be put away in their respective places.

During one of these flinging episodes, I heard a little voice quietly say, "I hope I'm still necessary in your life."

I've reached the age where it's time to focus on the time I have left. All the unnecessary and peripheral things need to go. That takes focus.

First I have to decide exactly where I need to expend my energies. I've discovered that God has given me gifts He intends me to use to help others. Who can I help? What kind of help can I give them?

Next, I need to equip for that ministry. What do I need to learn? How do I need to change?

Then there is always the fear. What about the fear of rejection? I put words on paper. What makes me think someone else wants to read them? Am I being arrogant? I push past those thoughts and submit an article.

I'm taking this a day at a time, a prayer at a time, a new concept at a time. I have no idea how many years I have left, but God does, and He knows exactly what He wants accomplished with the time I have left.

Maybe I'll be another Grandma Moses and come into my prime in my 80s.

The process of simplifying removes the unnecessary to enable me to focus on the necessary. That's the plan for now.

Acts 20:24 (NIV)

"However, I consider my life worth nothing to me; my only aim is to finish the race and complete the task the Lord Jesus has given me."

No Longer Contained

We were working in the garage and had opened the door to get a little breeze. Our dog, Charlie, was safely contained in our fenced backyard. Then I heard the jingle of his collar coming from the driveway. By the time that thought registered, he strolled nonchalantly into the garage.

How?

John secured Charlie while I went to investigate.

The gate was wide open.

Now this gate is very difficult to open and close. Believe me, no dog could do it. I barely can. We had no idea how that gate got open and it gave me an uneasy feeling.

Who?

Why?

How?

Sometimes, we think we have a memory or action from the past securely fastened in a gated area of our mind. Then out of the blue, that memory is staring us in the face.

What caused the gate of your memory to open? What do you do with it once it's released? Do you even know what you have contained? Is it something from the past that needs to be dealt with now?

Acts 3:19 (AMP)

"So repent (change your mind and purpose); turn around and return [to God], that your sins may be erased (blotted out, wiped clean), that times of refreshing (of recovering from the effects of heat, of reviving with fresh air) may come from the presence of the Lord"

Passing Power

DRIVING ON TWO-LANE highways used to concern me. It took all the nerve I had to stick my nose out from behind a slow moving vehicle to see if I could pass. I needed a long straight stretch to have time to get out, pass, and tuck back in. Driving was what I did to get from point A to point B.

Then I purchased an Acura TL.

The first time I poked my nose out, waited for my chance, and then passed, I was aware something was drastically different. It was as though I had no sooner decided to pass than it had suddenly occurred. When I pushed on the accelerator, I had power. From that moment, driving became a delightful experience— even on two-lane roads,

Then there's the first half of my life. My two-lane highways concerned me. I occasionally stuck my nose out, but would quickly decide it was too dangerous out there and withdraw. I traveled from point A to point B with no joy or pleasure in living. The journey was a mandatory part of life.

Then I discovered that *God loves me.*

The first time I stuck my nose out, after that discovery, I had Someone right beside me, helping me sail past the obstacle in my road. The problem didn't go away, but now I had access to a Power I had never had before. No longer did life consist of trying to get from point A to point B.

Since I tapped into an unending Source of power, my life has become a delightful road trip.

Acts 1:8a (NLT)
"But you will receive power when the Holy Spirit comes upon you."

Not So Bad After All

WITH MUSIC PLAYING, AND me singing along, I was the only car driving down Highway 395. Beautiful mountains, trees, and little streams provided a backdrop for the wonderful time I was having.

I came around a curve just as two motorcycles pulled onto the highway from the side of the road. I slowed to give them time to get up to speed.

No problem, I thought. *These are motorcycles. I'll be eating their dust in no time.*

Didn't happen.

They barely accelerated to the speed limit, and occasionally dropped below. They had spaced themselves one behind the other, and there was no room to pass them one at a time. I would have to pass both, but the road was continuous curves with a solid yellow line on my side.

I checked the speedometer—45 MPH. What was their problem?

At this rate, it would take much longer to reach my destination. More than that, they had taken away my pleasure in driving. Not only was I going slowly, but I was on alert in case one of them bobbled.

Finally, they pulled over at a turnout and allowed me to pass. I resumed the music, singing, and having a blast . . . until I rounded a curve and found myself behind a logging truck.

I groaned.

As I drove 25 MPH behind the truck, I recalled the frustration I'd felt at the slowness of the 45 MPH motorcycles. That had been better than this.

For mile after mile, I drove at 25 MPH, mentally tapping my fingers with impatience. There was no passing lane and no turnout big enough for the truck to pull over.

I glanced in my rearview mirror, expecting to see my motorcycle friends. They would catch up soon.

After what seemed like hours, the truck turned on its right signal, slowed almost to a stop, and then turned off the road.

Liberated, I picked up speed, but before I returned to my music, my thoughts turned to life. How like humans to think we have it bad. Maybe we want a bigger house, or perhaps we have a health issue we're struggling with. Then just around the curve, we see a larger family than ours, and they are living in a smaller house than we have. Or maybe we meet someone with a terminal illness.

Maybe we don't have it so bad after all.

Philippians 4:11
"I've learned by now to be quite content whatever my circumstances."

Rest Area

John and I did quite a bit of traveling by car, and I've seen my share of rest areas. Most are clean, serviceable, and modern enough. They have separate sides for men and women, with regular flush toilets and sinks. Many of them even have vending machines. Sometimes, on heavy travel weekends, they have a table set up with cookies and coffee. A few are slick and ultramodern.

Then there is the one I stopped at on a trip down Highway 395.

The sign on the highway declared it a "rest area," so imagine my surprise when I discovered an outhouse with a motorcycle in front. I had to wait my turn.

Rest areas are there to provide a basic service. They are a place to go to the bathroom. If you are desperate enough, as I was, you are grateful for an outhouse.

As I traveled on down the road, my thoughts turned to churches. They could be seen as rest areas. They are there to provide a basic service—a community of caring Christians. They come in all sizes and shapes. Some are not much more than the outhouse style, with wooden floors, one room, and hard wooden benches. Most are modern buildings, with carpet, cushioned pews or chairs, and separate rooms for classes. A few are like the Crystal Cathedral, made of glass and stained windows, with room for thousands of people.

If your need for community is strong, the building does not matter. The "outhouse" church can provide the love of God just as well as (or sometimes better than) the ultramodern ones.

On our journey of life, we all need a rest area.

Acts 2:44-45

"And all the believers lived in a wonderful harmony, holding everything in common. They sold whatever they owned and pooled their resources so that each person's need was met."

Kennel Life or Freedom?

MY HUSBAND AND I sat by the fire pit, feet propped on the edge, as we watched three-year old Charlie romp in the backyard. He would grab his toy, run back and forth on the grass, collapse to chew frantically, bounce up, and repeat the running. Occasionally he would skid to a halt between our chairs and bless us with his panting tongue hanging out.

In other words, he was having a blast.

So different from the dog we brought home three months earlier. That Charlie never pounced, ran, or came to stand beside us. He eyed us warily from his chosen corner. If he was lying down, and one of us stood to do something, Charlie was instantly on the alert, standing and watching.

The first time we tried to put Charlie in the car, John had to lift him in. Charlie didn't know how to ride. He kept falling over and slipping off the seat. There was no head hanging out the window.

We had a thoroughly traumatized dog.

Charlie had been a stud dog at a kennel and we can only surmise that he lived in a cage. Apparently he had no social contact with people. We were told he never barked. He existed from day to day, serving only one purpose.

As I watched him at play, I thought of the before and after, and I could identify. I used to be like that traumatized dog. The Joy I was before eyed everyone warily. People meant hurting. I had no social skills; no running and playing. My life was to serve one purpose—being religious.

But a loving God rescued me from that cage.

You should see the "after" Joy. I no longer strive to be religious, but am now free to live life to the fullest.

In other words, I'm having a blast.

John 16:23-24

"This is what I want you to do: Ask the Father for whatever is in keeping with the things I've revealed to you. Ask in my name, according to my will, and he'll most certainly give it to you. Your joy will be a river overflowing its banks!"

Flapping Zigzag Lines

JOHN AND I TRAVELED almost every weekend, him on his motorcycle (a new one which must be ridden) and me driving a car (not new, but must be driven). On one trip, headed west on I-84 about an hour from home, I noticed something flapping under the windshield wiper.

Weird. How could something suddenly be under there?

It continued flapping as I headed north on I-82. It had been faint before, but became darker and more defined.

Those jagged edges look like pinking shears.

Gradually, I saw the same jagged edges above the windshield wiper. It looked like a shark's mouth quickly opening and closing.

I'm losing my eyesight. I need to stop driving.

I pulled to the side of the road. My plan had been to exit the freeway and meet John in Hermiston for lunch, but now the Columbia River was ahead. I had missed the exit. I was afraid.

With cars zooming past and my hazard lights blinking, I tested my eyesight. Closing first one eye and then the other, I came to the conclusion there was a problem with both eyes. I closed my eyes and the flapping zigzag lines continued, growing larger and more vivid.

What is happening?

I prayed . . . at first more like begging. *Please touch my eyes.*

As I sat there, not knowing what to do next, the intensity of the zigzag lines began to fade. Slowly, the picture in my head of shark's teeth biting began to shrink. Then it was gone.

Thank you, God.

By the time I could turn around on the freeway, my hands were no longer shaking. As I drove toward Hermiston, that's when the nausea hit. I was so scared, it had made me sick to my stomach.

When we arrived home, I went straight to my friend Google. Typing in "jagged lines in vision," I immediately had many choices. As I read, I understood that I was not the only one in the world that this had happened to. It's a type of migraine and causes nausea.

My issue with all of this was my reaction. If I believe that God cares for me (which I do), and I believe that He is working all things together for my good (which I do), then why did I get so upset?

And so I've pondered . . . do I really believe? If so, where was my faith?

Romans 8:26 (NLT)

"And the Holy Spirit helps us in our weakness. For example, we don't know what God wants us to pray for. But the Holy Spirit prays for us with groanings that cannot be expressed in words."

Imposter in the Midst

THE DEFINITION OF "COUSIN" is: the child of your aunt or uncle. That would entail knowing either my mother or father's sisters and brothers. Never having met my father, or anyone on his side of the family, that leaves him out. My mother had many siblings. One time, in my early life, I met one of her brothers and three of her sisters. I have no idea who their children are.

My three oldest sisters were pregnant when my mother was expecting me. Two of my nieces were born during the same month as me. Three months later, I gained a nephew. I grew up with the thirteen children of my older sisters and brother. I thought we were cousins.

I spent a lot of time with one of the nieces born in the same month as me. Pictures taken in the early 1940s show us together at almost every family gathering. I was the one with the bows in my hair—one on each side of my head. She was the knock-kneed one.

Two of my brothers-in-law were amateur photographers, so many pictures were taken of the family. We were arranged in all types of groups: all the women, all the men, each family. Then it was time for the picture of all the cousins. Since I thought I was one, I would run to join them as they posed. Without fail, some adult in the family would escort me from the group. I didn't belong.

I looked like the cousins. I acted like the cousins. I was the same age as the cousins. Why wasn't I one?

As I grew older, I began to understand that I was the aunt, but I sure felt like a cousin.

Then came the day the cousins rebelled. They would not have their picture taken without me in it. All the explaining went unheeded. I was one of them!

In the midst of the pictures of the cousins, there is an imposter. She's the one with the bows on her head.

Matthew 19:14 (NLT)
"But Jesus said, "Let the children come to me. Don't stop them! For the Kingdom of Heaven belongs to those who are like these children.""

Tell Your Face

I recognized the voice immediately and instantly had a very non-Christian thought. *Please don't let her see me.*

I knew this lady from church. I had heard others speak highly of all the activities she was involved in. Yet, in my few encounters with her, I seemed to have a different opinion, which I kept to myself. Only God and I knew that I went out of my way to avoid her in the church hallways.

And now she was right there in the appliance store where I worked as a bookkeeper.

My office was in a separate room at the back of the store, without a door to shut. Chances are she would never know I was back there, but I wondered what kind of interaction there would be between her and the salesperson.

I went back to my work.

Later, as my co-workers reviewed the day, they mentioned the one lady who was difficult to deal with. They asked me if I knew her.

"Yes. She's a member of my church."

"She goes to church? I've never seen a face that sour on a Christian. She should tell her face."

I have never seen this lady smile. Her mouth is perpetually turned down at the corners. She looks like she is in a constant state of irritation.

Her visit to the store happened years ago, and yet I remember the comment my co-worker made: *she should tell her face.*

It made me very aware of the face I show to the world. Do I look like someone who has a wonderful life? If someone were to find out I attend church, would my face make them want to go there and discover what makes me so happy?

What is your face saying about you?

Matthew 6:16 (AMP)
". . . do not look gloomy and sour and dreary like the hypocrites . . ."

Simple Fix

Porokeratosis. *Say what?*

That's what my mind said when the podiatrist gave me that diagnosis.

"But it's a simple fix," he said. "We excise the plug, and the pain will go away."

I didn't know this man, but I trusted he knew what he was talking about.

I walk two miles every morning, but over a few weeks, the bottom of my foot had become more and more painful. With my fingers, I could feel a hard lump. It was like a piece of glass poking me with each step. So I purchased some donut-hole pads from Dr. Scholl, but the pain had overridden the padding.

I decided to soak my foot and take care of that lump myself. Didn't work.

That's how I ended up walking into the doctor's office at 3:15 PM that Monday. The doctor was correct. It was a simple fix. He picked up a surgical knife, scraped, poked, and prodded the bottom of my foot, and the plug popped out.

I walked out of the doctor's office at 3:30 PM that same day. Simple fix.

As I walked pain free on the treadmill later that week, my thoughts turned to how simple it is to become a Christ-follower. Just as the doctor removed the painful plug on my foot, Christ removes the painful baggage we carry with us.

But in the same way I tried other things before I finally went to the doctor, we try to take care of our own pain. Some of us eat; others drink or do drugs.

All we have to do is turn to him. He says, "It's a simple fix. Trust in Me. Give Me all your pain." He gently removes our plugs, whatever they may be. All He asks in return is that we live for Him, letting Him guide us through life.

I may have to return to the podiatrist at some point. He told me the porokeratosis tends to come back. That's the physical realm, but in the spiritual realm, one time is enough. My simple fix with Jesus has lasted over forty years and counting.

Matthew 11:28-30

"Are you tired? Worn out? Burned out on religion? Come to me. Get away with me and you'll recover your life. I'll show you how to take a real rest. Walk with me and work with me—watch how I do it. Learn the unforced rhythms of grace. I won't lay anything heavy or ill-fitting on you. Keep company with me and you'll learn to live freely and lightly."

Repurposed

With the crowd flowing all around me, I stood and looked at the sign on the vendor booth. Reused . . . Recycled . . . Repurposed. Those three words struck a chord in my soul. I had lived them, but it was the last word that filled me with a sense of accomplishment. I *now* live a repurposed life.

I grew up with the understanding I was good for cleaning the house, cooking the food, doing the ironing, having babies, separating myself from all the evil people in my neighborhood and school, and attending church every time the door was open. If I could perform all that perfectly, then I *might* make it to heaven.

When I met Jesus, I discovered I had received false information. He only cared about my heart. My neighbors or classmates could not create an adverse effect on it. I was the only one who could inflict damage. If I gave my heart to Jesus, He would protect it.

So began my repurposed life.

There was one more line on that sign. It said, ". . . into functional art." As I looked at the wares on display, I wasn't too sure about that declaration, but I was sure about what I had become—a functional human being whose new purpose was to care about others and show them God's love.

2 Corinthians 5:17

"Now we look inside, and what we see is that anyone united with the Messiah gets a fresh start, is created new. The old life is gone; a new life burgeons!"

To Save a Life

SHE WAS 36 HOURS old. I was 16.

The doctor placed her in my arms, patted me on the back and said, "She may die before you get there. If she does, do not react."

Arden, the baby's father, would probably have a car wreck. The mother was still hospitalized due to complications from childbirth. My fiancé and I knew them from church; so when the baby needed to be transported from a hospital in Emporia, Kansas, to a hospital in Kansas City, Missouri, Arden chose us to ride with him.

I was in the back seat holding Trudy, the newborn. As the car flew down the Interstate through the darkness, I watched every breath she took, waiting for her little chest to stop rising and falling.

We later discovered, after myriad tests, that no food had ever entered Trudy's stomach. We didn't know it in the car that night, but the baby was starving to death.

I had thought my job would be over when we reached the Kansas City hospital. I was sure someone from the hospital would relieve me of my burden.

Not so.

Still very aware of every breath Trudy took, we raced through the hallways to the right section.

Now, *surely*, someone would take this baby from my arms and help her.

Still didn't happen.

No one seemed to understand this was an emergency. Paperwork came next.

Another hour passed before we were ushered into a room where a surgical team was gathered. Only then was Trudy released into their care.

My arms were suddenly very empty.

I will never forget the urgency I felt as I carried out my commission. The fact that Arden was driving like a maniac, at a speed the car could barely maintain, did not faze me. Knowing my mother had condemned me to hell for going out of town—perhaps overnight—with two men, neither of whom were my husband, did not stop me from focusing on the need at hand. Trudy.

She lived.

As I remember that night, my thoughts turn to another commission I have been given as a Christ-follower. I am to go out and tell others about a way of life that gives them freedom and choices . . . and peace . . . and hope . . . and salvation. When opposition comes, or it seems the situation is out of control, my love and caring still needs to be focused on that person in need.

And so I ask, how well am I doing?

What about you?

Matthew 28:18

"Jesus, undeterred, went right ahead and gave his charge: 'God authorized and commanded me to commission you: Go out and train everyone you meet, far and near, in this way of life, marking them by baptism in the threefold name: Father, Son, and Holy Spirit."

Scanning for a Cloud

I SCANNED THE HORIZON, and in Kansas that's a lot to scan. No clouds in sight. But springtime in tornado alley ensured that soon—if not today then tomorrow—there would be a cloud.

It was inevitable.

I had been taught what type of cloud was dangerous, the kind that could become a swirling, sucking column moving across the ground and destroying everything in its path.

So I lived in fear.

Sure enough, a cloud would appear way out in the west. As it grew higher and wider, I knew we were in for it. Our two-room upstairs apartment could not protect us from the danger.

I felt vulnerable.

In the year 2000, I returned to that Kansas house where I'd lived in the 50s. A lot of storms have buffeted it over the years, but it's still standing.

I know people who live life like the young girl I was. It might be medical clouds they scan for. Is this lump cancer? Is this pain arthritis? Does this headache mean a tumor?

Or perhaps it's a financial cloud they dread. Will I be able to pay my bills next month? How will I feed my children if I get laid off? Will I lose my house?

They live in fear and feel vulnerable.

In the years after my first husband left, I lived like that. When your mind is constantly flooded with stress—real or imagined—it causes illness that requires you to spend money you don't have. That, in turn, leads to more stress. It's a vicious cycle.

I lived in fear and felt vulnerable.

Then I discovered there was a different way to live. My days did not have to be consumed with dread and uncertainty. Even if there was a cloud on the horizon, I knew I would be protected.

I found God—not the one my mother taught me about, but one who cared about my fears and vulnerabilities. He held out His hands, and one by one, I gave my anxieties and insecurities to Him.

In my seven decades on this earth, I've been buffeted by a lot of storms, but I'm still standing—not by my own power but by utilizing the Power within me.

Psalm 107:29-30

"Then you called out to God in your desperate condition; he got you out in the nick of time. He quieted the wind down to a whisper, put a muzzle on all the big waves. And you were so glad when the storm died down, and he led you safely back to harbor. So thank God for his marvelous love . . ."

Where's the Power Outlet?

OUR REFRIGERATOR DIDN'T PROVIDE enough space for our food needs. We needed a back-up, so I measured the garage wall between the laundry room door and the heating/cooling system. Leaving space for the light switch to be accessible, I had twenty-three inches available for a small refrigerator.

Even though I worked at an appliance store, it was not a size we kept in stock, so it had to be special ordered. In the meantime, cans of pop, bottles of water, and tea continued to be stored on wire shelving in that space.

The refrigerator was to be delivered on Thursday, so on Tuesday night I cleaned off the shelving and moved it out of the way. Imagine my surprise when I discovered there was no power outlet behind that shelf. Now what?

I stretched an extension cord from another wall to allow the refrigerator to receive power. Then I contacted the builder of our home to come out and provide direction on what can be plugged where. That blue extension cord across the floor was a temporary measure only.

As I worked in the garage, I thought about the various types of people in the world. There are those who assume they have power available. Their philosophy is to move some issues around in their life and they'll be able to discover a power outlet.

Some spend their whole life never moving anything, in the hope that power will be there when they need it.

Others have realized that even though they may rearrange their life—new wife, new house, new job—what they really have is an extension cord strung through their relationships. This is not a true fix.

Christ-followers know exactly where the power outlet is. No extension cord is needed. This outlet can handle the big jobs, as well as the small ones. And His power never goes out, not even when a tornado hits. Believe me, I know. I've been through some life tornadoes and have relied totally on the power available in Christ.

Psalm 147:5 (NLT)

"How great is our Lord! His power is absolute! His understanding is beyond comprehension."

Tough Love

THE CHOICE WAS HIS. He could stay in my room while I ironed or go outside. But Charlie wanted to be with John, so he refused to obey the command to stay.

Tail wagging, he headed down the hall to find my husband, who was getting ready to leave the house. John promptly escorted Charlie to the back door and put him outside.

Immediately, Charlie was at my sliding screen door begging to come in, whining to be in the very place he had only minutes before rejected.

Isn't that just like humans?

We give our children choices—this or that.

They choose a different path, but all too soon they return, begging to be given what they were originally offered. In the same way Charlie didn't know that John was leaving, our children don't know all the facts we've obtained from a lifetime of living.

I ignored Charlie's whining. He had his chance. I've also been known to ignore my children's whining. It's called "tough love."

And now I get to the heavy part . . . isn't that how we are with God?

We have myriad choices, but we think we have a better plan, and off we go on our own. When it doesn't work out, we come back . . . whining.

God is very good at tough love.

Hebrews 12:6

"It's the child he loves that he disciplines; the child he embraces, he also corrects."

Relentless Noise

MY WORLD WAS FILLED with sound. Before I opened my eyes in the morning, my ears were already working. They had no choice. The noise filled the room.

Taking a walk provided no relief. It was constant.

Trying to sleep was the worst of all. Amazed, I watched as my husband was lulled to sleep by the pulsing tide.

Our motel room was on the beach. As the tide came in, the lapping water inched closer and closer. Thank goodness we weren't on the first floor.

I longed for quiet. Occasionally, the waves would crash with such a crack that I jumped in my restless sleep. Couldn't it stop for a while?

And that is the dilemma. Did I *truly* want the tides to cease? What havoc that would bring to the whole world.

When I had small children, there were times when the constant movement and noise of my little girls seemed endless. When they learned to talk, words flowed with regularity, like the waves of the ocean.

Can't they just please be quiet for a while? The thought would flit through my mind, but did I really want that?

In the same way that stopping the tides would bring havoc to our world, the quietness of children would break my heart. I've witnessed a toddler in a coma. The parents longed to hear that relentless childish noise again.

Maybe your spouse talks a lot. Do you really want them to stop? Think about how quiet it would be if they were suddenly gone.

Perhaps your work environment is noisy. It would definitely be quieter if you didn't work, but is that what you truly want?

The ocean didn't get me. As I write, I'm inside a house with twelve-inch walls that keep out most of the noise. But I still remember the lesson I learned as I listened to the relentless rhythm of our world.

Psalm 95:5 (NLT)

"The sea belongs to Him, for He made it. His hands formed the dry land, too."

Reflection

As I TURNED WEST to leave the gym parking lot, the brilliant glow through my windshield deprived me of the ability to see.

Should I mention it was 6:00 AM? The sun was rising, but a large house with many east-facing windows was in my line of sight. I quickly adjusted the direction I was looking and traveled on home.

But those golden glowing windows stayed with me (imprinted on my eyes and in my thoughts) as I mulled over the significance of that powerful reflection.

More pondering over the day led me to check the dictionary for the definition of *reflection:* "An image given back from a reflecting surface; a reflected counterpart."

Which led me to look up the word *counterpart:* "One that has the same functions and characteristics as another."

As a Christ-follower, I am called to reflect Christ.

In our world today, there are many who call themselves Christians, but their actions do not reflect Christ. Many times, in their process of picketing, proclaiming untruths, and judging others, they reflect evil.

No wonder so many people want nothing to do with Christians.

So I ask myself: What am I reflecting? Is it a tiny light? Is there a light at all? What more do I need to learn, do, or be to reflect the dazzling light that shines on me?

Exodus 34:33-35 (NIV)

"When Moses finished speaking to them, he put a veil over his face. But whenever he entered the Lord's presence to speak with Him, he removed the veil until he came out. And when he came out and told the Israelites what he had been commanded, they saw that his face was radiant. Then Moses would put the veil back over his face until he went in to speak with the Lord."

Vision Problems

"JUST REST YOUR CHIN right here. Now lean forward so your forehead touches here. Look at the chart in front of you and tell me which row you can read."

"Which chart? I see two."

That's how my visit to the eye doctor went. I'd been having trouble with my vision for a few weeks, so asked for an emergency appointment. I already knew I was seeing double—not side by side, but one above the other.

"OK, tell me when they come together."

I waited and waited for that to happen. Finally there was only one. Then we could begin to work on the new prescription for my lens.

In our world today, there are many religions. Instead of seeing double, we see myriad options to worship, and the object of that adoration has many names. In essence, the leader holds a chart before his followers and asks them to focus their vision on what *he says* is right.

Sometimes we ask, "Which chart?"

For years, I tried to adjust my vision to a chart held up by my leader. It was a chart that only vaguely resembled the Bible, but since it was the only chart I had ever seen, I read all the lines with gusto. I had twenty-twenty vision.

In my 30s, I began to have conversations with other people about my chart. That's when I discovered the plethora of charts in the world. Was mine the real one?

I visited several churches as I tried to make sure my spiritual eyesight was OK. I waited and waited for my vision to come into focus.

Then came the day my quest ended and my eyesight merged into one belief. I could read all the lines and had twenty-twenty vision.

His name is Jesus, and He is the perfect prescription for vision problems.

Mark 8:23-25

"[Jesus] asked, 'Do you see anything?'

He looked up. 'I see men. They look like walking trees.' So Jesus laid hands on his eyes again. The man looked hard and realized that he had recovered perfect sight, saw everything in bright, twenty-twenty focus."

Urgent

IT CAME IN THE mail—an envelope with the word URGENT in red letters on the outside. Did I win the lottery? No, I hadn't played. So what was so very urgent? Should I rip the envelope open in anticipation of some wonderful news that would change my life?

No such news. Instead, I was told my magazine subscription was about to expire . . . a magazine I had already decided not to renew.

We throw words around like super, awesome, and urgent, but they don't live up to the hype they proclaim. Super means *very large or powerful.* When is the last time you had a very large or powerful experience? How many events in your life can you truly say were awesome, which means *extremely impressive or extraordinary?*

And then we get to the word that started this whole thing . . . urgent. I would think something that *needs immediate action,* which is the definition of the word, would not be sent by snail mail. When that envelope was placed in my mailbox, a few days later, was it still urgent?

There is a time and place to use words like these. When my daughter skated through a plate glass window and lay bleeding on the concrete, the word *urgent* applied. Those working over her body understood the urgency.

Pastor Chuck Swindoll says the only time we should use the word *awesome* is to describe God. If you've met Him, you understand. I think the word *super* fits God, too, but in my day-to-day life, I truly don't fix awesome meals or do a super job with the housework.

When God gets involved, well that's a whole different story. I've experienced some very large and powerful changes in my life that are extremely impressive and extraordinary. When I hit bottom, I turned to God and He took immediate action.

He understands the meaning of the word *urgent.*

Psalms 63:1 (NIV)
"You, God, are my God, earnestly I seek you; I thirst for you, my whole being longs for you, in a dry and parched land where there is no water."

Straw or Hay

As I pulled into the parking lot of where I worked, the signs at the feed store next door caught my attention. There were two stacks of bailed material. One stack had a sign that said "straw." The other stack's sign said "hay." They looked exactly alike. I climbed from my car and moved closer, trying to discern the difference. To my eye, they were the same.

I worked all day, but when it came time to leave, I took one last look at the two stacks and then took a picture. I was intrigued. When I got home, I searched for the definitions of straw and hay.

Straw is the stalk of grain after threshing. It's used for bedding or packing. Beneath that definition was the word "chaff." So I was off and running, looking up that word. Chaff is the seed covering and other debris separated from the seed when grain is threshed.

Next stop, hay, which I discovered is grass that has been mowed and cured for fodder. That led me to look up the word fodder, which is something fed to domestic animals; an especially coarse food for cattle, horses or sheep.

While all this was banging around in my head, I remembered scriptures that talked about chaff and threshing floors, causing separation.

Matthew 3:12 (NLT)

"He is ready to separate the chaff from the wheat with his winnowing fork. Then He will clean up the threshing area, gathering the wheat into His barn but burning the chaff with never-ending fire."

The worthless chaff is burned.

Hay is useful and straw is worthless, but to the untrained eye, they look exactly the same.

I can look, act, talk, dress, and read my Bible like a Christ-follower. My money can be used to help the poor and I can spend my time doing good works. To the untrained eye, I look like a Christ-follower.

But I know if I'm straw or hay . . . and so does Jesus.

Mandatory Evacuation

THE WATERS ARE RISING, the rain relentless, and the orders are given: mandatory evacuation. Or the wildfires are burning out of control, the air is filled with smoke and ash, and soon it will be your house that's burning. Lately, it's been hurricanes Harvey, Irma, and Maria that have caused much devastation. Do you flee?

We've seen pictures in the newspapers and on television of women and children being helped into boats, escaping with just the clothes on their backs and possibly a few keepsakes. We've watched as men weep when the fires destroy years of memories and treasures. Do you stay?

A mandatory evacuation is exactly that—mandatory. Supposedly you have no choice, but we've watched on television as men and women alike announce they will not flee the hurricane. "We've lived through all the others and we're not leaving now." When people refuse to leave, they are told, "You will be on your own. We cannot help you.

The mandatory part of the evacuation is not always so mandatory. However, there is one that we will all face. Sometimes we have warning that it's coming; other times it's sudden. No matter how much others may want to help us, this is one evacuation we must do on our own, and we won't be taking any keepsakes. Everything will be left behind. When God says, "It's time," we won't have a choice.

Following a natural disaster, people deal with power outages, no water to drink, and empty grocery shelves. We've been warned to always have an emergency supply of flashlights, batteries, bottled water, canned food (and a can opener), and whatever else we may need to get through a time of being cut off from supplies.

We can physically prepare for emergencies, and we also have a way to get ready for that final mandatory evacuation. Christ-followers will be glad to assist you, and reading your Bible will give you insight and guidance. A minister would be willing and able to counsel you . . . but Jesus is always right there.

If you ask for help, He will gladly give it.

John 5:24
"It's urgent that you listen carefully to this: Anyone here who believes what I am saying right now and aligns himself with the Father, who has in fact put me in charge, has at this very moment the real, lasting life . . ."

It's a Gradual Process

IT HAPPENS SO GRADUALLY that you don't realize it's occurring. Over time you accept it, and then one day, it becomes too much. You decide to do something about it. You go to the eye doctor.

I would catch myself tilting my head, trying to find a position where my glasses would actually help me read those words. My eyes were in a constant squint, trying to get numbers in focus. No matter how hard I concentrated, those two images wouldn't merge into one. And then there was the watering of my eyes, which necessitated always having a Kleenex nearby. Then I got my new lenses.

The technician took my glasses, removed the old lenses, inserted the new ones, and placed my "new" glasses on my nose. "There, how do those feel?"

Feeling wasn't the issue. I could see the edges on the counter, the edges on the doorway. Everything had edges. Down the hallway was a sign that said *Restroom*. I could read it without any tilting or squinting.

On the drive home, I read all the signs along the way and thought of how gradually changes can occur in other areas of our lives. We gain five pounds this year and another five pounds next year. Slowly, we change clothes size, until one day we realize we've gained fifty pounds.

Or maybe it's the marriage that's been changing over the years. The spark left a long time ago. Conversation has become stilted. You no longer engage in the same activities, living separate lives. And there's that person at work who actually listens to you when you talk. Your marriage is dying a slow death.

I consulted an eye doctor for my problem.

There are dietitians, doctors, and programs available to help with weight loss. Even though the answer is to eat less, it's not that simple.

Pastors and marriage counselors are available to help your dying marriage, but it may need something as elementary as paying attention to what's happening.

If you catch yourself tilting, squinting, or straining at life, it's time to seek help.

1 Corinthians 10:23 (NLT)
"You say, 'I am allowed to do anything'—but not everything is good for you. You say, 'I am allowed to do anything'—but not everything is beneficial."

Life in a Car Wash

I LINED MY CAR tires up with the track . . . or at least I tried to. The young man standing in front of my car motioned for me to turn a little. Soon I felt my car slide into the narrow slot. Placing it in neutral and removing my foot from the brake, I was ready for my trip through the car wash.

The suds on my windows were so thick I could not see out. I was isolated from the outside world in a cocoon of soap, metal, and glass. Next came the thick strips of material slapping against my car, knocking off dirt and grime. Slowly, the car inched forward to the forceful water spray.

Even if I wanted to get out, I couldn't. I thought. *I'm trapped in here.*

I began to feel the buffeting of the blowers aimed to dry my car. As the windshield cleared, I could see the end of the tunnel. Young men with cloths surrounded me and began the final drying.

Then that track my tire had been resting on spit me out into the parking lot and my journey through the car wash was complete.

Have you ever felt that way about your life? I have.

At a young age, I was placed on a rigid track that propelled me in only one direction. I lived an isolated life in a cocoon spun from threads of dogma. I was trapped. Thoughts of escape eluded me. This was my lot in life.

An arranged marriage in my teen years only changed the location of the cocoon. Rule after rule was added to my ever-growing list, slapping against my spirit and knocking off any creative or personal thoughts.

And the buffeting . . . it was relentless.

I saw no end to my tunnel. Have you ever been there?

Even though I was unaware of His presence, God was there in that cocoon with me, infusing me with strength and preparing me for when I would be spit out into life. I look back on that time and marvel at God's provision for me, emotionally and mentally.

He will do the same for you.

Luke 12:28 (NLT)

"And if God cares so wonderfully for flowers that are here today and thrown into the fire tomorrow, he will certainly care for you. Why do you have so little faith?"

Pain Tolerance

IT HADN'T STARTED OUT that way. I'd gone to the dentist to get a filling, but the more the dentist worked on my tooth, the more sounds he emitted. Finally he said, "This tooth has metastasized from the inside. We are going to have to do a root canal."

Metastasized? Root canal? Were these words I understood?

He explained the decay had started inside my tooth and spread to the outside. A filling would not work.

"Does a root canal hurt?"

"Yes."

"How long does it hurt?"

"Not very long."

"OK, go ahead."

Since I have a reaction to the deadening used when working on teeth, I received no shot. I had given him permission to continue working on me without any anesthetic, and I can attest to the fact that root canals do, indeed, hurt.

Then he said, "I've never been able to do this before. I can ask you if I got it all." As he probed into the depth of my root, I jerked, thereby letting him know he *hadn't* gotten it all. I don't recommend getting a root canal without deadening.

How many times do we start out with a certain end in mind, but halfway into the situation, it changes. Due to ignorance or fear, we continue in the same direction, even though the outcome will not be at all what we anticipated.

The new job may sound great on paper or at the job interview, but after you quit your current job, move to another city, and ensconce yourself in your new office, you discover there are some issues you hadn't counted on. It's too late to go back. So you say to yourself, *OK, we'll just go ahead.* The results can be painful.

You buy a house, the market tanks, and you struggle to make house payments. The value of houses in your neighborhood drops. Soon you owe more than the house is worth. Do you still say, *OK, we'll just go ahead*? Being upside down in your mortgage hurts.

Even though we don't see persecution of Christ-followers in the United States, there are people in other countries who are beaten and tortured for their beliefs. They lose their freedom, their families, and their health. Being a true believer to the very end hurts.

It's all a matter of pain tolerance. How's yours?

John 15:18, 21 (NASB)

"If the world hates you, you know that it has hated Me before it hated you . . . But all these things they will do to you for My name's sake, because they do not know the One who sent Me."

Two Lives ... Two Deaths

THE OCTOBER 6, 2011 edition of *USA Today* carried a front-page picture of Steve Jobs. More than one page was dedicated to telling the story of his life in the technical world.

As I read the words, I searched for some information about his personal life. Was he married? Did he have children? But his story was about money and inventions. Buried deep on the second page was a personal paragraph. Yes, Steve Jobs was married and had four children.

More technical information was given, and then a surprise portion. He was born to unwed parents and adopted out. At one time, Steve had lived in a commune and become a Buddhist. By age 25, he was a self-made millionaire and the world would soon know his name.

The very same paper carried another story of life and death. It was on the third page, tucked inside a story about someone else. An inset showed a small picture of Rev. Shuttlesworth, who had died the day before.

I had never heard of him.

Rev. Shuttlesworth was born in Alabama and became a pastor of the Bethel Baptist Church in Birmingham. Very active in the civil rights movement, his life was constantly in danger. Once, he escaped unhurt when his house had been blown up. A police office at the scene (who was a member of the Ku Klux Klan) told him he needed to get out of town as quickly as possible. Rev. Shuttlesworth's answer: "I am not leaving. I wasn't saved to run."

He helped organize the Freedom Rides that challenged segregation in the South, and he preached his final sermon at the age of 84. Rev. Shuttleworth was 89 when he died.

In 2008, the Birmingham Airport's name was officially changed to Birmingham-Shuttlesworth International Airport.

Two very different lives.

Our technical world would not be where we are today without the creative mind of Steve Jobs. I used my iPad to search for information for this article. My iPhone is in my pocket. These words are being typed on a laptop. Hooray for technology.

Yet, where would the civil rights movement be today without the brave people who fought unbelievable hatred and archaic laws so that one day a black man could attain the status of President of the United States?

It matters not if we are white or black, illegitimate or legitimate, wealthy or poor. When death comes, all that matters is that we are ready.

God doesn't play favorites.

Isaiah 26:4-6

"People with their minds set on you, you keep completely whole, steady on their feet, because they keep at it and don't quit. Depend on God and keep at it because in the Lord God you have a sure thing."

Time Change

IT'S SO EASY IN the spring when we move our clocks forward one hour. On our non-digital clock, I take that hour hand, move it clockwise around the face, and we're done. But in the fall, when we move our clocks back one hour, that's a whole different story.

Moving the hour hand counterclockwise would damage the internal workings of the clock. Since it is designed to soften its tone at 10:00 PM and resume the loudness at 6:00 AM, that means I have to move the hour hand clockwise, full circle, 23 times, stopping to allow it to chime each hour.

Do you know how long that takes?

As I stood in front of the clock, patiently waiting for another hour to chime, I thought about how change is sometimes easy. When we moved to our new house, it was easy to change my route from home to work. When the weather gets colder, it's easy to change the clothes I wear from summer to winter.

But most personal changes take time and patience. We don't always want to make that effort, so we take the shortcut . . . move the hand counterclockwise and end up with a lot of damage to our internal workings.

The news headlines are full of stories about people who took the easy way and thought they would get away with it. When a marriage hits a rocky place, the easy way out is a divorce. It requires patience to work through the issues, one at a time.

Thanks to patience, I now have a clock that chimes the correct time on the hour. In the same way, couples who patiently work through their issues will end up with a strong relationship that keeps them in tune with each other.

1 Corinthians 1:10b

"You must get along with each other. You must learn to be considerate of one another, cultivating a life in common."

Irrelevant

IT SEEMED IRRELEVANT. IT was such a small window, set high up on the wall. So when we had window coverings installed in our new home, we placed blinds in every window but that one.

During the summer months, as I worked at my computer, I enjoyed looking out at the blue sky and puffy clouds, but by late fall, I had a problem. At certain time of day, when I sat at my desk, the sun shone in my face, which made it impossible to see the screen.

I tried to plan my day around the issue by avoiding the computer during that hour, but finally, I resorted to placing a box and a pillow in the window to block the sun.

How would I explain a box and pillow in my window?

So we had the window-covering people come back to measure, order, and install a little blind. If the sun begins to shine in my face, I simply use the cord hanging down at the side of the blind and shift the slats upward.

Why did I wait so long to do that?

Isn't that like life? Some small action or word can seem irrelevant. We enjoy our world, but all the time we're aware that there is an issue. It may only happen occasionally, so is it really worth the effort to try and remedy it? We alter our day to avoid someone. Or we change our behavior when we are around a certain person. We use boxes and pillows to avoid the issue.

Why not take care of it? In most cases, a fix is available. It might cost you something—time or money—but it will make a huge difference in your life.

Proverbs 27:17

"You use steel to sharpen steel, and one friend sharpens another."

Shame on Me

It was Thanksgiving Sunday morning and I was ready for church. I entered full of gratitude for all of God's blessings, one of which was with me that morning. My daughter, Lorri, had come home for Thanksgiving.

I found a row toward the front of the church, saved a seat on the aisle for John to sit in after he finished his ushering duties, and let Lorri go in the row before me.

As we stood to sing, a man took John's place beside me. I busied myself with asking Lorri to move over and sliding my coat over one chair. Lorri leaned over and said, "Mom, shouldn't we say something to him?"

Conviction washed over me as Lorri reached across and took his hand in welcome. For the first time since this whole scenario began, I looked at him. As we made eye contact, his words hit me like a brick.

"Is this a problem? Should I move somewhere else?"

Shame on me.

I smiled, took his hand, and assured him all was well—at least, that was, between him and me. I wasn't feeling too well in my soul.

During our time of greeting, I discovered this was his first time at our church. I had been his first encounter.

More shame on me.

As I asked for forgiveness from God, I prayed that this man could get past me and enjoy his time at our church.

At the end of the service, the elders and their spouses go to the front of the church for anyone who needs prayer. As John and I walked to stand by the platform, I thought, *I'm up here to pray with others when I'm busy with my own failure.*

I didn't make it back to my seat in time to say anything more to the man, but Lorri did. He told her he was from the Mission, and he said he had enjoyed his time with us.

Our church has a heart for the Mission. On Sunday mornings we send a bus there to pick up the people who want to come to church. He had come on the bus that morning. On arrival, he had watched the service on the screen in the mezzanine. Then, when he had decided it was safe enough, he'd slipped inside and taken John's seat.

Shame on me.

Matthew 25:35-36

"I was hungry and you fed me, I was thirsty and you gave me a drink, I was homeless and you gave me a room, I was shivering and you gave me clothes, I was sick and you stopped to visit, I was in prison and you came to me."

Old Programming

I BOUGHT GAS FOR my car this morning. I've been performing that duty for over 40 years. Yet each time, for an instant, my mind flies back to the first time I accomplished that task. Up until then, I had been programmed to believe that pumping gas was way beyond my capabilities.

That first time, as I pulled into the service station, I was overwhelmed with all that needed to be done. The correct distance from the pump . . . pulling up to the right position for the hose to reach the car ... knowing how to open the gas tank . . . making the gas actually pump through the hose. All these thoughts flooded my mind. My heart pounded. Was I about to make a fool of myself?

For years I had believed my old programming that said I was incapable of such a complex procedure. Today, so many years later, it seemed so simple.

We all have old programming. My list was long and most of it had to do with religion. It's not easy to overcome beliefs that have been pounded into your very core. It took time, and a lot of effort on my part, to change some very basic concepts about God and me.

Maybe you're dealing with some old programming, or are you even aware that you're operating under that old system? What kind of reactions do you have? Are they in response to what you believe, or to what you've been told to believe? Sometimes it's tough to separate the two.

Perhaps you're in the process of programming someone, probably your child. What are you entering into their system? Is it something they will have to work to overcome?

I learned to take each situation one at a time. Then I would observe my reactions and thoughts.

The next step was to decide if I wanted to change my behavior. That's when the hard work began. I apologized often to my children, sometimes changing my answer mid-stream.

I had a lot of old programming, but with God's help, it's now a distant memory.

Romans 12:1-2

". . . God helping you: Take your everyday, ordinary life—your sleeping, eating, going-to-work, and walking-around life—and place it before God as an offering . . . You'll be changed from the inside out."

God Connection Thermostat

I SAT IN MY room writing, fingers flying over the keys. Gradually, they moved slower and slower because they were getting cold. The cold weather had just begun and the heat had only been on a few days. *Maybe there's something wrong with the furnace. But there sure shouldn't be.* We had only lived in our new house for 18 months. The furnace should last longer than that before breaking.

My thoughts continued as the words flowed to the screen, until my brain was empty and fingers felt frozen. I checked the programmable thermostat. Even though it was in the 30s outside, the furnace was set for only 55. *What's up with that?*

Then I remembered back to the end of the last cold season. The temperature outside had been warming and our house was well insulated, so I had lowered the temperature setting.

The furnace was operating *exactly* as I had told it to.

Sometimes life is like that. We are so busy flying around town—running errands, going to work, homework with the kids . . . even church business—that we don't realize we are getting cold in our spirit. Gradually, we begin to notice our responses to others seem short and not so sweet.

Life continues, but something is missing, something that used to feel warm and loving. That's when we need to check our connection with God. One thing is for sure; He will always operate *exactly* as He has said He will. If we have lost our warmth, it will never be His fault.

What is your God connection thermostat set for? Sometimes? Maybe tomorrow? After the holidays? Or today and every day?

Check it out.

Hebrews 4:15-16 (NIV)
"For we do not have a high priest who is unable to empathize with our weaknesses, but we have one who has been tempted in every way, just as we are—yet he did not sin. Let us then approach God's throne of grace with confidence, so that we may receive mercy and find grace to help us in our time of need."

That's the Way He Works

THE WORDS OF THE song made me think of all my blessings. That's when I thought of the $100 bill tucked in my purse—my Christmas bonus. My needs were abundantly taken care of and I had money to spend.

Memories moved through my mind of the years when my needs weren't met. *There may be someone here today whose life is like that.* I replayed that thought. *What could I do for someone here today?*

"There is that $100 bill tucked away in your purse."

That's when my conversation with God began. *Yes, there may be someone here who needs help financially, but there are hundreds of people here. How could I possibly find the one who needs it? If there is someone here who needs my $100, then you are going to have to show me.*

The sermon was wonderful, with many thought-provoking illustrations and scriptures. Yet my mind kept returning to my $100 bill.

At the end of the service, John took my hand and we walked to the front to join the other elders and their spouses. It was time to pray for the needs of the congregation.

I saw two women inch their way through the people on their row. They headed toward the front, started to walk past us, and then turned and moved to stand before us.

"She doesn't speak English," the older lady explained, "so I'm here to tell you what she needs prayer for. She's trying to get to Oregon to her children for Christmas."

I looked at the younger lady. Such sad eyes. My heart did a little lurch.

We placed our hands on their shoulders and my husband prayed that God would help her find a way to get to her children.

Then church was over, and suddenly there was a friend asking me for someone's address.

"Sorry," I said as I reached for my purse, "I'm on a mission. Can you wait a minute?"

I walked across the aisle, took the younger lady's hand, placed my $100 bill there and curled her fingers around it. She nodded her head. Did she even understand what I had given her? Getting the attention of the older lady, I explained to her what I had done. Her exuberant reaction nearly knocked me off my feet.

With tears in my eyes, I returned to where my husband and friend stood waiting. Would that $100 bill help her get home to her children?

"It's not your $100 bill," I felt God say. "It was always Mine. You've done your part. Leave the rest to Me."

That's the way He works.

Romans 9:18

"God has the first word, initiating the action in which we play our part for good or ill."

If It Be Your Will

MANY YEARS AGO, I was invited to join in prayer with a group of people from the church I had recently begun attending. We gathered at the hospital bedside of one of their own who was very ill. Fervent petitions for healing ascended. Then I opened my mouth. It was my turn. I thought I knew how to pray, but as I finished with my words, there was dead silence. Immediately, everyone filed out of the room until we were out of earshot of the sick one. That's when they let me have it.

"What kind of Christian are you?"

"Where is your faith?"

"You just undid all of our prayers in there."

"Why would you say 'If it be Your will?' You know it *is* His will. Now she won't be healed."

I didn't attend that church very long.

I know what it is like to be desperate for an answer to prayer, to want to tell God exactly how He should respond, and I do believe He *can* heal. I've seen it happen in my own family. But the way I see it, it takes a lot more faith to say, "If it be Your will."

I would like for all of my days to be filled with sunshine, calm, excellent health, good finances, lots to eat, and everyone liking me, but I know that is not realistic. Some days are cloudy and rainy—both outside and inside my life. For someone my age, I'm in fairly good health, but I have some issues. Right now my bills are paid, but life holds no guarantees.

And I already know some people don't like me. They told me so.

The longing of my heart is that each day I will be able to say, "If it be Your will."

James 4:13-15

"And now I have a word for you who brashly announce, 'Today—at the latest, tomorrow—we're off to such and such a city for the year. We're going to start a business and make a lot of money.' You don't know the first thing about tomorrow. You're nothing but a wisp of fog, catching a brief bit of sun before disappearing. Instead, make it a habit to say, 'If the Master wills it and we're still alive, we'll do this or that.'"

Two Vessels and a Choice

THE PICTURE OF CARNIVAL Corporation's giant cruise ship *Costa Concordia* lying on its side was disturbing. That's not supposed to happen, and I'm sure the over 4,000 people on board felt the same way.

In a matter of minutes, eating was forgotten and survival was foremost. It cost a lot of money to be aboard that vessel. You would think that payment would cover being safe at the dinner table.

The world watched as the tragedy unfolded.

The next Sunday, our pastor spoke of Noah and his faithfulness. He was told to build a large sea-going vessel. There would be no charge for climbing on board, other than a belief that God meant what He said.

The world of Noah's day watched as he worked to build this giant container that could float, but only eight people were inside when God shut the door.

The *Costa Concordia* was equipped with all the latest in technology . . . the ark had none. Entertainment abounded on board the cruise sheep . . . feeding animals and mucking out their stalls awaited those on the ark. And the food . . . oh the food . . . lavish and in abundance for the passengers on that fated ship. Not so much on the ark.

The *Costa Concordia* had Carnival Corporation's guarantee of a good time. The ark had God's guarantee that you would live if you climbed on board.

In our world, the majority of people are willing to pay big money to enjoy glitter and opulence. Instant gratification is the goal. Some of us are willing to postpone our rewards while we do God's work, knowing we can trust His guarantee of heaven.

John 14:2-3 (NIV)

"My Father's house has many rooms; if that were not so, would I have told you that I am going there to prepare a place for you? And if I go and prepare a place for you, I will come back and take you to be with me that you also may be where I am."

The Soft Sound of Humming

My world was full of sound. Chuck Swindoll's voice came through my headset, expounding on the word of God as I walked on the treadmill.

The gym's radio was doing what it does best, blaring obnoxious music.

To my right, two treadmills down, two ladies talked and laughed.

I heard the clank of free weights, followed by the thud as they were dropped to the floor.

Yet I could hear humming.

To my left, two treadmills over, a lady walked steadily, holding on to the machine. Her eyes were closed and she was softly humming. I knew the song. Amazed I could hear her above all the other noise, I forgot Chuck as I listened to song after song. She was in her own world, unaware of the affect she was having on me.

That's a perfect example of how I desire my Christ-like life to be.

Our world is so full of chaos, noise, and activity that the soft sound of a Christ-like spirit is difficult to hear. Some of us blare our song like the obnoxious music from the radio. Others laugh and talk about surface things, never really saying anything important. There are also those who are focused only on building themselves up. They go through life lifting the weights of Bible study, and more Bible study, but never really touching the life of another.

Then there is the person who loves God and others, who softly hums in the background, a song about being real and caring for people.

That's who I strive to be.

1 Peter 3:4 (NIV)
"Your beauty should not come from outward adornment, such as elaborate hairstyles and the wearing of gold jewelry or fine clothes. Rather, it should be that of your inner self, the unfading beauty of a gentle and quiet spirit, which is of great worth in God's sight."

One Bad Apple

IT WAS A WEEKLY date, our trip to Costco. I'm not sure I would ever have gone there, except it was so important to John. The ritual became so ingrained that I no longer asked "Why?" Just "When?"

He gets lost in the "techie" section and I spend time at the book table. When we join up again, it's time to select our groceries.

One time, I selected some Gala apples in a plastic container that's kind of like an egg carton, with separate cups for each apple. Later, when it was time to place the apples on the check out conveyor belt, I noticed one apple was a different color than the rest. One push and I could tell that apple was bad, through and through.

I exchanged the container for one with all good apples, but I kept thinking about that one bad apple.

No matter where we go in life—work, school, or church—there will usually be at least one bad apple. That plastic apple container was designed to prevent any apples from touching. Therefore, the one bad apple was not able to contaminate any of the other apples.

As Christians, we have the same type of safeguard—a buffer from the bad apples. We are never commanded to keep ourselves separate from the non-Christian, but to keep ourselves protected. When we keep our mind on Him, He provides the barrier that prevents any corruption from occurring.

Ephesians 6:10-17 (NLT)

"A final word: Be strong in the Lord and in his mighty power. Put on all of God's armor so that you will be able to stand firm against all strategies of the devil."

Unraveling

I'VE BEEN CROCHETING FOR almost 70 years. My projects have included many afghans for both babies and adults. At the age of 12, I crocheted a dress for a one-year-old. Shawls, tablecloths, dishcloths, scarves, and hats are some of my finished pieces. I've used very thin yarn, and I've also used yarn so bulky that I had to buy an oversized crochet hook.

In all those projects, not one of them has been unblemished. When you crochet, you make mistakes. It's easy to be several rows along, only to look back and notice an error. Thankfully, it's easy to unravel something that's been crocheted—a quick pull and all the stitches disappear and become yarn again.

If the stitches have been in place for a while before the error is noticed, the yarn may not lay straight once it's unraveled. You might end up with a pile of crinkly yarn, but you can still return to the point of the error and re-do the stitches.

In my 70-plus years, I've made *life* mistakes too. The older I get, the quicker I am to realize I've made an error in judgment. It's fairly easy to make amends and resume any damaged relationship, but I've decided it's easier to not make the mistake in the first place. So I try to watch what I say and do.

It's the mistakes that lie dormant for years that are harder to repair. It's not as simple as pulling on the end of the yarn and unraveling back to the point of the error. Sometimes it's hard to even find the end to pull on.

Other times, the mistake has been there so long it's almost impossible to separate the rows of yarn. The threads seem to have melded together. In crocheting, there have been times where I've had to cut the yarn, tie a knot, and continue on.

As I look back at my life, I'm pleased to be able to say that I have repaired most of the errors. Some will never be fixed, and I have had to learn to live with that.

I know of some work that still needs to be done, but I'm not sure how to accomplish it and may have to cut those ties. Perhaps tying a knot will help. When you do that, the finished project will have a bump in it, a reminder of your mistake.

Crocheting is a relaxing pastime. I have a feeling of accomplishment when I complete a project. As I look at the relationships in my life, most of them bring a feeling of relaxation and accomplishment, too.

I'm sure I will keep crocheting until my fingers can no longer hold the crochet hook. In the same way, I'm sure I will keep working on the relationships in my life until my last breath.

In crocheting and in life, God has helped me create some beautiful projects.

Philippians 4:2

"I urge Euodia and Syntyche to iron out their differences and make up. God doesn't want his children holding grudges."

The Tongue

IT'S EVERYWHERE—ON TELEVISION, in the newspaper, in magazines, on the radio, and even mentioned at church. Valentine's Day. The focus is on what to get *her* for this special day . . . something that will show his undying love.

So who decided Valentine's Day was only for the female? Don't the guys deserve a show of love, too?

This brings me to the crux of this article. It's fairly easy to spend money and buy me something, but words are so much more important to me. Words that let me know I matter to him . . . I'm important in his life . . . that he cares about my happiness.

The tongue has the ability to embed words in our minds . . . words that encourage us and give us warm fuzzies, or words that destroy any hope we may have for our future.

Chuck Swindoll once spoke of a man I'll call Bill. At an early age, Bill's father told him he would never be more than a bum. Now in his 60s, Bill is wealthy, his home filled with expensive artifacts, but that is still not good enough. Bill is always seeking the next big purchase . . . still trying to prove to his dead father that he's not a bum.

A counselor at school told one of my loved ones they would never be good for anything but washing dishes. Words like that can crush a spirit. Words spoken to me as a child held me in a dark prison for years.

We are in control of our tongue. Think about the words you speak. It doesn't take many to bless or destroy.

Choose carefully.

James 3:5 (NLT)
"In the same way, the tongue is a small thing that makes grand speeches.
But a tiny spark can set a great forest on fire."

Inner Beauty

THE WORDS I HEARD in the television commercial resonated in my head. A well-known actress, comedian, and television host proclaimed that *inner beauty is important, but not nearly as important as outer beauty.*

How surface is that?

Did she really believe that? What about the cosmetic company proclaiming that? Do they even care about the potential damage inflicted by that premise?

I've observed the women in my life as I go through my days. My convictions have been affirmed. Inner beauty is far more important than outer beauty.

Oh, I believe if the house needs to be painted, then paint it. Now an image of Tammy Faye Bakker just flew through my head—no, not that much paint.

Who is the real you? Cosmetics can't change that.

We've all known a woman who looked beautiful until she opened her mouth. Sometimes it's the airhead who shows up; other times it's Miss Foul Mouth. No amount of covering on the outside will fix that.

I've known women who, by today's standards, are not beautiful, but they know exactly what they look like and who they are. It's delightful to be in their presence. Their inner beauty glows.

Inner beauty or outer beauty . . . you choose.

1 Peter 3:3-4
"What matters is not your outer appearance—the styling of your hair, the jewelry you wear, the cut of your clothes—but your inner disposition. Cultivate inner beauty, the gentle, gracious kind that God delights in."

People Watching

At first I didn't understand what was happening. Why were these people looking at me and holding their Costco cards in my direction?

It was chilly and breezy that day, and I had been sick for two weeks. When we went to Costco, John let me out at the doorway and then went to park. I stepped inside to wait for him.

The people entering the warehouse thought I worked for Costco. They were verifying their membership by showing me their cards.

When I realized what was occurring, I didn't move. It was fun to watch them when they figured out they had shown their membership card to the wrong person. Some stopped in their tracks, looking from me to the real employee.

It was a great people-watching experiment.

I love to watch people and contemplate what's going on in their lives. Sometimes I have to give myself a "Gibbs slap" to stop my negative critique of their clothing choice or body adornment. Many times I pick up signals of pain or loneliness. No two are the same.

As I watch other people, they are probably watching me. What signals do I give off? Do I have a wall up? Am I so focused on my own agenda I don't even acknowledge them? Does my face say, *Leave me alone?*

Everyone has a story. What are you telling?

Romans 14:1b
"Remember, they have their own history to deal with. Treat them gently."

TBR

As I read Robin Lee Hatcher's blog one morning, my mind traveled back over my life and my love of books. As a child who was not allowed to do anything, reading was my entertainment and escape. In my first marriage I again turned to reading to bring any comfort to my life.

Books are my friends.

That's why it was extremely difficult to sort through and give away so many books before we moved to our new home. For many of the books on my shelves today, I can remember where I purchased them and, perhaps, where I sat as I enjoyed reading.

I always have a few books on hand . . . waiting for me to discover what they hold within their pages.

Robin's blog that day gave a name to that pile of books: the TBR pile . . . to be read. Looking at my pile of unread books gives me warm fuzzies. I feel safe and secure in the fact I will not run out of reading material.

As I thought about the TBR acronym, I realized I needed to see people as unopened books ready for reading. I can remember where I met my friends and the conversations we've had. I would never be able to sort through them and give some away, so many wonderful memories of places and conversations.

But there will always be new people just waiting for me to meet them. Waiting to get acquainted and to learn their story.

That TBR pile is endless.

Proverbs 17:17

"Friends love through all kinds of weather, and families stick together in all kinds of trouble."

To the Rescue

THE CAR AND MOTORCYCLE collided and burst into flames. The 21-year-old man who had been on the motorcycle now lay unconscious under the burning car.

In the scene shown repeatedly on television, bystanders rushed to help. The first few people could not lift the car, but more men and women hurried to place their hands on the side of the vehicle and assist in the lifting. Even though there was imminent danger of explosion, there were soon enough good Samaritans to raise the car off the young man, enabling him to be pulled to safety.

As I watched the rescue unfold, I thought of the people in my life that had helped assist me. No one made them do it. They saw the peril I was in and came to my aid.

A brother who drove across two states to sit on my front porch and give me clear counsel . . . advice I never would have sought.

A different brother who placed his arms around me as he stood in my living room and said, "There's something terribly wrong in this home." Until then, I'd had no idea the issues were visible to anyone else.

A pastor who understood I was going under, asked what my name was, and then continued to talk to me like I was a real person . . . not invisible.

A different pastor who helped me understand I had value, even though I was a battered and bruised specimen of a human being.

My list could go on and on.

I don't know which side of this scenario describes you. Today you may be in need of aid. People truly do care and want to help, but you have to be willing to accept their assistance. Pride can get in the way. Would you really rather stay under that burning car than suffer the indignity of being pulled out by one leg . . . your lifeless body sprawled on the street for the world to see?

None of us know when there might be a collision, either one we witness or one which involves us, but we are all in this life together.

Luke 10:33-34 (NLT)

"Then a despised Samaritan came along, and when he saw the man, he felt compassion for him. Going over to him, the Samaritan soothed his wounds with olive oil and wine and bandaged them. Then he put the man on his own donkey and took him to an inn, where he took care of him."

Scleroderma

SHE STRUGGLED TO KEEP her composure, tears leaking from her eyes. My heart broke as I listened to her words. She was a vibrant young lady with a supportive husband and two small boys, and she had been given a diagnosis of a disease with no specific treatment.

A life sentence.

Scleroderma is an autoimmune disorder in which the body's immune system mistakenly attacks and destroys healthy body tissue. As she talked, I remembered people I'd seen with frozen faces, unbending fingers, and thinning hair. *Has she seen those pictures?*

Some of the complications are life threatening: cancer, heart failure, high blood pressure, kidney failure, and colon issues. Her diagnosis was recent and she was still processing the news. Her emotions ran rampant and her face displayed fear, briefly anger, gratitude that it wasn't her children . . . and then fear again.

What I had to offer was a listening ear, hugs, and the promise of prayer. So she goes through my days with me. Each time she comes to mind, I shoot a prayer her way.

This is a journey I can't take for her. No one can.

As I thought about the progress of the disease—the hardening of the skin and possibly organs—my mind turned to some Christians I've known. My diagnosis would be spiritual scleroderma. Their faces do not radiate joy, but are frozen in a scowl. The most threatening complication of spiritual scleroderma is the hardening of their heart.

But that's not a life sentence. I know a great Physician who can soften any hard heart.

Ephesians 4:18 (NIV)

"They are darkened in their understanding and separated from the life of God because of the ignorance that is in them due to the hardening of their hearts."

Substitutes

IT WAS TIME TO do laundry. I gathered the dirty clothes and noticed my pajama top had been removed from the stack ready for washing. It was now across the room. Weird.

The minute my hand touched the fabric I knew something wasn't right. It was wet. Upon examination I discovered a large hole.

Charlie.

Charlie is such a good dog, but he loves to chew. Even so, after a year living with us, he had never chewed on any clothing.

I completed my laundry duties and dropped the whole issue. It was too late to discipline him now. I put it down to a random urge on his part.

The days passed and I began to notice little pieces of hard black rubber on the floor. I searched through the house to see what might be coming apart and even extended the search into the yard. I came up empty.

Then one morning, after eating my breakfast, I discovered a little piece of hard black rubber under my chair. Where were these pieces coming from? I'm not sure what drew my attention to my house shoes. They had a hard rubber bottom, and sure enough, the whole toe area on one of them was missing.

Charlie.

What was wrong with him? I keep my house shoes on a low shelf in the walk-in closet—not exactly lying around. Yet, he had gone out of his way to find them.

As I pondered what had changed in his life, I remembered how Charlie had destroyed his toy chewing bones with his strong teeth. I had found no replacements at the store. At the time, I'd thought, *He can do without them . . . can't he?*

Apparently not.

Humans are like that. As a foodaholic, I understand the need to search for a substitute for that three-layer chocolate cake. People are constantly searching for alternatives for their addictions. Some seek a replacement for their spouse, one that will make them happy.

Just as Charlie used my pajamas and house shoes for his need to chew, we have a need—an empty spot we are born with. Some people search their whole lives, using one substitute after another, trying to fill that empty spot.

Christ is the only answer. Substitutes just won't do.

John 3:36

"That is why whoever accepts and trusts the Son gets in on everything, life complete and forever! And that is also why the person who avoids and distrusts the Son is in the dark and doesn't see life. All he experiences of God is darkness, and an angry darkness at that."

Jigsaw Puzzles

Jigsaw puzzles are such fun and I'm good at them. They come in all shapes, sizes, and cuts. Some of them are not interlocking. Those pieces slide together and are the most difficult. When my daughters and I get together to spend a week, we work puzzles and make memories.

Imagine my delight when I discovered I could work puzzles on my iPad.

There are rules for putting together a puzzle. First you put all the edge together. That builds the framework for your picture. Of course, you must have in front of you the picture of the completed project. This helps you group colors and patterns, and enables you to work on small sections that can then be joined together to make a bigger section.

Before you know it, your puzzle is complete.

Life is like that, but not everyone understands about the framework for his or her existence. No one told me; therefore, it was impossible for me to make sense of all my pieces. The picture of the completed project of my life was all one color and none of the pieces were interlocking. I would think I had a piece that worked, but it would slide to a different spot.

I spent half my life trying to put that puzzle together.

Then I discovered the correct framework in a book called the Bible. As I read its words, the completed picture came forth. One color was about loving, another about forgiving. Patterns emerged for parenting, marriage, and even growing old.

I've completed several sections of my life puzzle and am working on joining them together to enable me to become more like Jesus.

Hebrews 6:1-3

"So come on, let's leave the preschool fingerpainting exercises on Christ and get on with the grand work of art. Grow up in Christ. The basic foundational truths are in place: turning your back on "salvation by self-help" and turning in trust toward God; baptismal instructions; laying on of hands; resurrection of the dead; eternal judgment. God helping us, we'll stay true to all that. But there's so much more. Let's get on with it!"

WD-40

THE DRIVER'S SIDE DOOR hinge on my car needed to be oiled, but it wasn't a good time to stop and oil it when I was getting into my car. When I returned home, tired from work or with groceries, that wasn't a good time either. So I put up with the noise and it being hard to open.

Plus, there's the fact that WD-40 *really* stinks.

Then it was time for an oil change. I scheduled the appointment, took the car by Meyer's Auto Tech, waited the allotted time for the work to be completed, paid my bill, and walked to my car. With my hand on the door handle, I gave a giant pull on the door. If I had been standing any closer to the car, my legs would have received damage. The door swung open smoothly and completely. The odor of WD-40 reached my nostrils. They had oiled my door.

Once behind the steering wheel, I easily pulled the door shut. *I'll have to get used to that.*

But I quickly forgot.

When I got home, I opened the door with force. The heavy door swung smoothly to its widest point and pulled me right out.

Why did I put up with such annoyances for so long?

In other areas of life, I've done the same thing. It's so much easier to put up with the irritations—people who drag you down with their negativity, ones who prefer to play the victim, others who think God put them in charge—than it is to confront. It's never the right time, and besides, it really stinks to get in someone's face and speak the truth.

As I've discovered who I am and who God wants me to be, I've learned about tough love. Sometimes others have no idea how they come across. Some make it very clear they like being that way. When I speak the truth, at least I've done my part. I've sprayed some care and love on them.

Thank goodness for God's love and WD-40.

1 Corinthians 4:14

"I'm not writing all this as a neighborhood scold just to make you feel rotten. I'm writing as a father to you, my children. I love you and want you to grow up well, not spoiled."

Scorpions

A POST ON FACEBOOK caught my attention. A friend was having problems with scorpions on their living room floor and on their necks. Instantly, I was transported back to my time spent living in Stinnett, Texas.

We, too, had lived with scorpions.

At the age of three, one of my daughters was taught to turn her house shoes upside down and shake them before she put them on in the morning. Scorpions loved to sleep in shoes (or whatever it was they did in there).

Checking for scorpions became a way of life—one I did not enjoy.

As a Christ-follower, I've had to learn about shaking off the scorpions—pride, judgmental attitude, busyness . . . the list goes on. These attitudes sneak up on you while you are sleeping. It's not enjoyable to have to check for those scorpions, but very necessary. If I miss checking for a day, that might be the very time one has shown up.

Not only do I need to be aware of attacks on me personally, but I also want to warn others.

Certain species of scorpions have the capability of killing a human being.

Certain attitudes can cause grave damage to my spirit and could be fatal if allowed to continue.

The control of scorpions can be difficult and time consuming, but it can be done. First you have to thoroughly clean your home. There are insecticidal dusts or sprays that finish the job. I love it that one of the insecticide products is called *Demon WP*.

It's the same when checking for spiritual scorpions. First, I must clean house. It's amazing what I can find in the corners, but I pull out my Demon WP, better known as the Holy Spirit, and do a little spraying.

Works every time.

Luke 10:19 (NASB)

"Behold, I have given you authority to tread on serpents and scorpions, and over all the power of the enemy, and nothing will injure you."

Voice From the Back Seat

I HAD STRUGGLED TO find this job and I couldn't afford to lose it. Therefore, when I received a call from the school that Lorri was throwing up and I needed to come and get her, the decision to leave work in the middle of the day caused me concern. My children came first, always, but so did feeding them.

I left work, drove to the school, and then took Lorri home.

"Take off your shoes and put on comfy clothes. I'll get you some 7-UP."

When I returned to her room, she was still exactly where I left her—no changing of clothes and no removing of shoes.

"Lorri, why didn't you do what I asked?"

"I can't bend over."

Red flags . . . waving high.

A few questions later, we headed for the car. This required a doctor's intervention. I made Lorri a bed in the back seat. Dr. Gustafson, or Gus Gus as my kids called him, was the next stop.

"God, you know I'm having a hard time. With their dad gone, I'm really struggling and very alone. Are you there? Please help me with Lorri. Something's seriously wrong. Give me the strength I need to go through this by myself."

"Everything will be OK."

I slammed on the brakes, my head whipping around to look in the back seat. "Who said that?"

Lorri lay perfectly quiet. No one else was there.

As I continued driving toward the doctor, I knew without any shadow of doubt that God had told me everything was going to be OK. I was also aware that assurance didn't mean she would live or die, but whatever happened, it would be OK.

That was the day we discovered Lorri has a very high pain tolerance. Her appendix was close to rupture. The emergency operation caught it in time.

And everything was OK.

Philippians 4:13 (NLT)
"For I can do everything through Christ, who gives me strength."

Moment of Truth

THE NIPPY NIGHTS WERE a faded memory. Little green buds poked up from the ground and on the tree branches. Spring had arrived.

Which led me to that awful moment of truth—will everything still fit?

Each change of season brings with it the task of exchanging clothes that keep you warm, for clothes that will help you stay cool, or the other way around. When it came time to sort, I placed some clothes in a Goodwill pile and others in a container waiting for next year.

Each change of season I have a dream that I will try them on and, low and behold, they are too big. Yet, for several seasons, that hasn't happened. Standing on the scales ahead of time told me they would fit the same as last year.

One can always change eating habits and hope.

As I sorted through my clothes, my mind wandered back to my life the last time I took these clothes out. Had there been any change in my attitudes, my walk with Christ, my relationship with loved ones? Or was I the same size?

There is always that awful moment of truth when I step on the scales of Christ-follower guidelines—the Bible—and check my progress. Just as, some years, the clothes are a little (or a lot) too tight, sometimes I fall far short in representing Christ.

But I can do more than hope for a difference next time. I can change my habits, work on my attitudes, and ask for God's help.

One day it will be my season, my last moment of truth.

Matthew 25:21 (NIV)

"His master replied, 'Well done, good and faithful servant! You have been faithful with a few things; I will put you in charge of many things. Come and share your master's happiness!'"

Tornado Country

In the distance, the clouds lit up with lightning, but no thunder rolled. John and I sat on our patio enjoying one of the first warm enough evenings to sit outside. As we talked, the flashes of light grew brighter and closer.

Then we heard the first peal of thunder.

"If I still lived in Kansas, now is when I would start being afraid and looking for shelter. I'm sure glad I don't live in tornado country any more."

Perfectly at peace about the storm building outside, I went to bed.

The next morning at the gym, I heard snatches of conversation about the storm. At work, coworkers talked of the wind, pouring rain, blinding lightning flashes, and cracking thunder. The morning paper had pictures of trees on houses and a trampoline that had been moved from one backyard to the roof of the house next door.

I slept through it all.

Before I understood who God is, I lived in perpetual "tornado" country, never knowing when one was going to hit. My life was full of wind, pouring rain, blinding lightning, and cracking thunder . . . all designed to make me fearful of God and the destruction He could cause in my life.

But I've moved from "tornado" country into the peace of God's love where I rest securely.

Hebrews 4:6 (NLT)
"So God's rest is there for people to enter, but those who first heard this good news failed to enter because they disobeyed God."

Just Call Me a Mule

WHEN I STOPPED RIDING behind my husband on the motorcycle, I became very useful to the motorcycle club. I love to drive my car and I enjoy spending time outdoors, even camping in a tent. Attending a motorcycle rally in a beautiful part of the country allows me to do all of that and more.

The members of the club call me their *mule*.

If I attend a rally, then my car is used to haul stuff—tents, sleeping bags, chairs, and other varied and assorted items. I meet with the group early in the morning, we have breakfast, and then my car is loaded with their things. I wave goodbye as they head out, then climb in my car for some fun time for me.

They like the twisties, and I like straight and fast. Works out just fine.

Then one day, my mule status changed to a more personal one. While at motorcycle training, my husband fell, landed on a large rock, and bruised his hip. It's hard to carry things when walking with a cane. So guess who carried everything then?

I'm a versatile *mule*.

My Bible tells me I'm to be another kind of mule, willing to carry another's burdens to help lighten their load. The Message Bible puts it this way: "Stoop down and reach out to those who are oppressed. Share their burdens . . ."

We all have cares and worries, but sometimes they become overwhelming. That's when the Christian *mule* steps in.

Galatians 6:2 (NIV)

"Carry each other's burdens, and in this way you will fulfill the law of Christ."

Percolating

SHE HAD STATED IT in passing . . . and then the conversation turned elsewhere. But I was still back at the statement: "So you've got some words up there," she pointed to my head, "that are percolating."

Funny word, *percolating*. It described exactly how my mind felt.

I've never liked coffee, never been able to get past the smell, but as a child, I remember my mother making coffee in a percolator. The heated water would be forced under pressure through the grounds into the pot. The finished product exhibited color, taste, aroma, and stimulating properties.

As a writer, I often feel the force of an idea seeping through my consciousness. After a time of percolating, I sit at a keyboard and the finished product flows through my fingers. It is my desire that my words contain color, taste, aroma, and stimulating properties—but I don't want to stop there.

As a Christ-follower, one who listens to sermons and reads the Bible, the force of that input needs to penetrate my very soul, percolate, and then emanate from my life in living color, taste, and winsome fragrance. I'm not finished yet, but I can exhibit to the world what it means to live an abundant life.

So far as I can tell, my percolator seems to be in working order.

John 16:23-24

"This is what I want you to do: Ask the Father for whatever is in keeping with the things I've revealed to you. Ask in my name, according to my will, and He'll most certainly give it to you. Your joy will be a river overflowing its banks!"

Reconciliation

ONE OF MY DUTIES, as a bookkeeper, is to reconcile the bank statement. To do this, I compare what the bank says happened with our money, to what my records say happened. If they agree, then the bank statement has been reconciled. I do this every month.

I can't imagine how difficult it would be if I waited a few months, or years, or even longer, to try and make those figures compatible. Without reconciliation, I would never know for sure how much money we had.

Yet, I see people all around me who have relationships that need to be reconciled. Marriages fail because the couple did not establish a consistent method to reconcile their issues. Friendships that were once close become strained and gradually cease to exist.

It takes time and discipline to reconcile my bank statement, but knowing where I stand financially is important to me, so I make that effort. Reconciling a relationship takes the same kind of time and discipline. It all depends on how important that relationship is to you.

Sometimes there are extenuating circumstances that prevent reconciliation. My mother was too old and set in her ways for us to negotiate one, and I had to accept that fact. Other times, mental illness may stand in the way.

Every month, it's a relief to know the bank balance is correct, but that does not compare to the satisfaction felt when a broken relationship has been reconciled.

Matthew 5:23-24 (NIV)

"Therefore, if you are offering your gift at the altar and there remember that your brother or sister has something against you, leave your gift there in front of the altar. First go and be reconciled to them; then come and offer your gift."

Lessons From Charlie

We taught our dog Charlie to talk to us before he received some benefit, such as a treat, meal, or a walk. If he barks, he loses. What we desired was a soft growling sound. Sometimes he works his mouth for several seconds before he emits any sound. Other times the movement ends with a whiny yawn.

One day, I placed his food in his dish, carried it into the room where he was, and waited for him to indicate he wanted it. First he ran back and forth, tail wagging furiously, looking at me the whole time.

That didn't get it.

Then he tried a series of short barks. I still stood holding his filled dish. I knew he wanted the food. All I required was that he ask. Not pace in agitation, not bark in demands, but ask.

How many times have I paced back and forth wanting something from God, but never really asked? Maybe I've used short, clipped sentences to make my demands known.

The God I know and love wants to give good things to me. He stands ready and waiting, but just as we don't give Charlie everything he asks for, such as food that wouldn't be good for him, God takes into consideration what is best for me.

Before God will acknowledge my request, I must stop my agitated thoughts, stop feeling He owes me, stop whining, and come into His presence with an unassuming attitude.

When Charlie finally asked nicely, I placed the dish full of dog food on the floor . . . and he began his meal, tail wagging with enjoyment. That brought a smile to my face.

I want to always ask in a way that makes God smile.

Proverbs 18:23
"The poor speak in soft supplications; the rich bark out answers."

The Waiting Place

When I worked as a nurse's aide in a nursing home, I was almost overwhelmed by the way the residents were treated there. It was all about money; no one saw those patients as human beings.

In the twelve months I was employed there, Anna had never had a visitor. When I had a break, I would sit by her bed and hold her hand. Paralyzed by a stroke, her eyes were the only part of her body that contained a spark of life. Now she was slowly dying

One day, with my shift over, I headed for the door to leave, but I overheard a conversation about Anna at the nurse's station. Plans were being made for a new patient who would occupy that room. The new patient's family had been called. It was only a matter of time for Anna.

Immediately, I made a u-turn, which caught the attention of the nursing supervisor.

"Where are you going?" she asked.

"To be with Anna."

"That's not part of your job," she said brusquely. "You can go on home."

"I don't want her to die alone," I said softly. "I will sit with her."

Anna heard me enter and her eyes locked with mine. She knew.

I sat down, took her lifeless hand in mine, and leaned close to her face. "Anna, I know you can hear me. I want you to know I'll be here with you."

Tears leaked out of her eyes and ran toward her ears. I wiped them away.

"Anna, do you know Jesus? Blink twice if the answer is yes."

Instantly. she closed her eyes and opened them twice.

"Then soon you'll be free of this body and be running and jumping down the streets of gold. Are you ready for that?"

Two blinks . . . and more tears down the cheeks. Once again I gently wiped them away. I had never done this before. A part of me wanted to leave the room and forget it was happening. But I could not leave her alone.

I sang softly and prayed, my eyes locked on hers. When they closed, my breath caught, but the rise and fall of her chest told me . . . not yet.

It didn't take long. Anna was ready and she gently slipped away.

I sat there in silence. In my mind, I saw Anna whole again. I had witnessed a wonderful passing, but selfishly, I hoped I would never end up like Anna—an active mind trapped in a lifeless body.

I prayed I would remember this moment of Anna's release.

Still holding her hand, my reverie was interrupted by the strident voice of the nursing supervisor. "Why didn't you tell us she died? We need to get this room stripped and disinfected. The new patient is arriving at eight."

I was ushered from the room as the flurry of activity began.

I wondered what they planned to do with Anna's body, but Anna no longer cared. She was free.

Hebrews 4:9-10 (AMP)

"So then, there is still awaiting a full and complete Sabbath-rest reserved for the people of God; for he who has once entered God's rest also has ceased from the weariness and pain of human labors . . ."

Travel Agents for Guilt Trips

I'M NOT SURE WHERE my mother received her training, but she had it down pat. "Shame on you for not cleaning your plate. There are children starving in China who would love to have that food."

So I cleaned my plate and weighed 140 pounds in grade school.

"Do you understand there are people who live below us in this building? Don't you care that your heavy footsteps across the floor just bothered them?"

So I basically tiptoed my way through life.

"How could you possibly think of wearing a skirt that short? You are supposed to be a Christian. What kind of message do you want to send to others?"

So my skirts and dresses never rose higher than my calf.

If I had a certain look on my face, I offended her and others. If I asked (once only) to listen to something other than sermons on the radio, again the Christian club came out. Only sinners would listen to anything else. God would be ashamed of me.

I lived my life under the cloud of guilt.

When I emerged from that life, I resigned as a travel agent. My children had already been on many guilt trips. We were through with that kind of traveling.

Guilt is a useless emotion. Even if you did do something wrong, you can't undo it. Repent and apologize, whatever you need to do. Then get on with life.

If someone else tries to manipulate you with guilt, surprise them. Don't take that trip.

Psalm 19:12-13

"Clean the slate, God, so we can start the day fresh! Keep me from stupid sins, from thinking I can take over your work. Then I can start this day sun-washed, scrubbed clean of the grime of sin."

Sunburned Forehead

I WAS ON VACATION in Tahoe, spending time with my daughters. We were busy seeing, doing, and talking. Then we took a break and sat on the deck at Starbucks.

Time passes quickly when you are enjoying yourself.

I failed to take into consideration that we were at 6,000 feet elevation and I am rarely in the sun. It never occurred to me, as we sat and visited, that my forehead was being baked.

I had a beet red forehead for several days after that, and then it peeled. Lovely.

How easy it is to get so involved in what we are doing that we lose focus on important things, like protecting ourselves from the damage being done by outside forces. We let the foul language from a television program wash over us as we sit unprotected in our spirit. We watch a movie without morals and forget that our soul is being burned.

There is a product called sunscreen. I've been using it since that fateful day. No more burning. As Christ-followers, we have a powerful Sunscreen that will protect us from those harmful rays of evil. But just as sunscreen wears off and you have to slather more on, we need to be in close contact with Christ as we go through our day.

Once or twice a year just won't cut it.

Proverbs 30:5

"Every promise of God proves true; he protects everyone who runs to him for help."

Stop, Look, and Listen

DO YOU REMEMBER THE railroad crossing signs that urged us to *Stop, Look, and Listen*? Not only cars, but people were also to *stop* before crossing the tracks. Yet people continue to think they can beat the train and try to cross in front of it, thus resulting in their death or disability.

What about the *look* part? After stopping a distance away from the tracks, we were to look both ways, searching for the telltale headlight of an oncoming train. Still, some people chose to ignore the warning.

And then there was the instruction to *listen*. That's why the train blows its whistle at the intersection. If the stop and look part didn't work, maybe the *listen* would cause the observer to stop before crossing.

When you arrive at a train crossing, you are required to make a decision.

Some decisions we face in life are as dangerous as a railroad crossing. Those decisions can impact our wellbeing, career, or relationships. If we follow the *Stop, Look and Listen* philosophy, we have a far better chance of crossing safely.

If we *stop* long enough to gather the needed information, we can make a much better decision. But the stopping needs to occur before we are on the tracks. It is just as important to *look* before moving onto the tracks. We must consider possible outcomes that will affect more than us. We need to understand the options, risks, and consequences if we choose to cross over. Finally, we need to *listen* to advice of others before we make a major decision. We need to hear their experiences and how the crossing affected them.

Have you arrived at a crossing in your life? Take the time to *Stop, Look, and Listen*.

Proverbs 2:2-3 (NLT)

"Tune your ears to wisdom, and concentrate on understanding. Cry out for insight and ask for understanding."

It's All About Me

BEFORE A TRIP TO Lake Tahoe, a friend told me to be sure to take the scenic drive around the south end of the lake. That way I would end up at the viewpoint overlooking Emerald Bay. So the very first day of vacation, that's exactly what we did.

We enjoyed the beautiful view of the bay, with its island in the middle and house at the top. It was just as my friend had said it would be.

A few days later, we took a two-hour cruise on the lake. One of the highlights of the trip was Emerald Bay. As we drew closer, I could see the island, and watched as the house on the top grew larger.

I decided I would take pictures, up close and personal, for my friend. He had only seen it from high above. I grabbed my iPhone from my pocket and clicked away. As we circled the island, our tour guide explained the house was built as a teahouse, complete with steps climbing the steep hillside to the top.

I was so pleased to know I would be able to show the pictures and tell the story to my friend.

I returned to a shaded area and pulled out my phone to view the pictures. Imagine my surprise when I saw twelve pictures of ME! The sun had been so bright that I couldn't see the screen. I didn't realize I'd pressed the button that switches the lens around so you can take a self-portrait. I had close ups of my eyes, nose, and mouth—twelve of them.

It was all about me.

Life can be like that. We have good intentions. We're busy doing something we say is for someone else. Yet, when we take a moment to stand back and look at the whole picture, all that activity has been to show others how good, how self-sacrificing, how benevolent, or how wonderful we are.

It's all about us.

What kind of pictures are you taking?

Romans 9:10b-11a (NLT)
"This message shows that God chooses people according to his own purposes; he calls people, but not according to their good or bad works."

What Direction Are You Traveling?

I KNOW THE SUN comes up in the east and sets in the west. So when I left home to drive south to John Day, Oregon, I knew I was driving south. Profound, huh?

As I drove along, I glanced at my GPS screen. It showed what highway I was on, where the filling stations and restaurants were, and any government property, state parks, rivers and lakes.

It also showed what direction I was going. I looked at the little arrow and it was pointing directly north. I quickly checked the highway sign. Had I made a wrong turn? How could I possibly be going north?

I wasn't.

Apparently, my GPS was no longer receiving a signal. I continued south on the highway, glancing occasionally at the GPS screen. Within minutes, the arrow magically switched to point south. Now the GPS and I agreed.

For so many years, I lived with absolutely no idea what direction I was traveling. My church told me I was going a certain direction, but years later, I discovered I had relied on a faulty system. Just as the GPS failed to provide correct directions for me as I drove, my church had failed to provide correct directions for me as I journeyed through life. I took them at their word instead of checking for myself.

I now know exactly what direction I am traveling.

It's nice to have a church home. I love having the fellowship of other believers. But when it comes to making sure I'm going the right direction, I don't turn to a human being for that guidance. I have a GPS that never fails.

Do you know what direction you are traveling?

Psalms 25:4 (NLT)
"Show me the right path, O Lord; point out the road for me to follow."

What a Surprise!

IT WAS A LOVELY evening. Our small group had gathered for a social in the backyard of the leader's home. The invite had said to bring our swimming suits because the pool was ready. So we did.

After cooling off in the water, it was time to eat. Tables were set up in the grass, each with its own umbrella to protect us from the sun. We filled our plates and moved to the tables with our food and drinks. Conversations abounded as each table discussed a different topic. Laughter and joking, stories about kids and trips, and then . . .

The sprinklers came on.

Shrieks filled the air as we made a mad dash to the concrete poolside. As we stood there, wet clothes and sodden food, the shock began to wear off. That wasn't exactly how we planned to end the meal, but all was good. No one was injured. There was plenty of food to re-fill the plates. And none of us melted.

It's the way things go sometimes. We're enjoying each day, taking time for friends and play. Then out of the blue, the sprinklers come on. Oh, not literally, but suddenly we're wet and sodden. We make a mental dash to safety, complete with complaining or discouragement. That wasn't how we planned it.

Sometimes the solution is as simple as turning off the sprinkler, but many times it takes a process of sorting, counseling, support of friends, and maybe laughter, to come to the understanding that we didn't melt. Tomorrow, or next week, or next month, life will go on and we will laugh again.

Luke 8:22-25

"One day he and his disciples got in a boat. A terrific storm came up suddenly on the lake. Water poured in, and they were about to capsize. They woke Jesus: 'Master, Master, we're going to drown!' Getting to his feet, he told the wind, 'Silence!' and the waves, 'Quiet down!' They did it. The lake became smooth as glass. Then he said to his disciples, 'Why can't you trust me?'"

The Plan

WHEN MY DAUGHTER, LORRI, moved from Oregon to Georgia, she drove all 3,366 miles—just her and two cats.

Before she left, she made a plan with the help of AAA. They provided detailed maps and directions. She knew where she would be stopping each night, how long she would drive each day, and when she would arrive in Georgia. I was given a copy of the map with the highlighted route so I could travel along with her.

It all looked great on paper.

Halfway through Day 1, Lorri's air conditioner quit working. This had not been mentioned in the plan, which was an oversight, since she was headed to Wyoming, Colorado, and Texas—places with daytime temperatures over 100. She sweltered across Wyoming and into Colorado, where she sought help from an uncle and his family.

They were unsuccessful, so after spending a night in southern Colorado, Lorri forged on through west Texas, the AAA plan all forgotten. Her goal now was San Antonio, where another uncle lived.

Part of her plan had been to listen to music and books on tape as she traveled, but with the windows down to get air movement, the road noise drowned out any chance of listening to anything.

Day 4 had been scheduled to get her to New Orleans, but she spent the day in San Antonio while repairs were made on her car. Lorri left San Antonio in the evening, and Day 4 blended into Day 5 as she drove through the night. She crossed Louisiana and Mississippi, and it was in Alabama that her air conditioner quit again.

On the evening of Day 5, Lorri reached her destination in Georgia.

Isn't that exactly how life is? We have a plan, a good one, all laid out. Maybe our plan is marriage and children, and then we are unable to get pregnant. Or perhaps attending college is the plan, but suddenly the funds dry up and it's necessary to get a job to help provide food for our family.

Life gives us no guarantees, but there is one Plan that is sure and guaranteed to work. With Christ as our guide, we can know each step of the way He is with us. Even though times look dark, He will lead us through the night, sometimes carrying us. As we journey, we can turn to Him—morning, noon and night.

When we reach our destination, He will be there to greet us with open arms.

Psalm 25:2, 4 (NLT)
"I trust in you, my God! . . . Show me the right path, O Lord; point out the road for me to follow."

No Connection

Brand new computer . . . check.

New wireless mouse . . . check.

New monitor . . . check.

New wireless keyboard . . . check.

Everything plugged in and ready to do great things, and then the words came up on the screen. No connection.

I had returned home from a weekend in Seaside. The car was unpacked, clothes were in the washer, and I sat at my desk ready to send out my blog. That's when I discovered I had no Internet connection.

Sunday evening passed . . . no connection.

Monday morning arrived and those words kept appearing on my computer screen.

Finally, when I came home from work that evening, my Internet was connected.

How frustrating and time wasting. There was so much I could have accomplished if I'd had a connection.

I've seen beautiful churches with wonderful sound systems, awesome video productions, energetic worship teams, and a pastor that speaks words to tickle the ears. People gather in the building, week after week, to fulfill their duty of attending church. They leave with a good feeling, but without a connection with Jesus, they have no power.

Others do not see a great God living through their lives, and they exist that way, day after day, week after week, month after month, and year after year.

How frustrating and time wasting. They could accomplish so much if only they had that connection.

Ephesians 4:15-16

"God wants us to grow up, to know the whole truth and tell it in love—like Christ in everything. We take our lead from Christ, who is the source of everything we do. He keeps us in step with each other. His very breath and blood flow through us, nourishing us so that we will grow up healthy in God, robust in love."

Sign Language

I sat in Starbucks watching a very unusual sight. At the bar by the window, with his back to me, a young man was Skyping. Now that's not all that uncommon, except for one thing—he was using sign language. I could see the screen on his computer and the other person was signing right back. They were communicating in their own special way. It was a very silent conversation that I could not understand.

I've pondered about a unique language I grew up with in church. In my earlier years, I listened to many conversations loaded with religious words that I understood because I had been trained in that vernacular. Words like:

Atonement
Blood of Christ
Heresy
Holiness
Messiah
New Covenant
Pentecost
Repentance
Sanctification

To anyone outside my religion, this was an unknown language.

Now, as a Christ-follower, I try to speak words that anyone can understand— simple words. My desire is for others to have a relationship with Jesus. Pious words are not needed for that to happen. Everyone understands words like:

Forgiveness
Love
Sorry

Are you still using sign language?

Colossians 4:6 (NLT)
"Let your conversation be gracious and attractive so that you will have the right response for everyone."

The Test

IN OVER 70 YEARS on this earth, I've had some hard tests and I've learned from them. I was raised to believe that worry and guilt showed others how much you wanted to please God, and I had those emotions down pat.

Then life happened.

My worry and guilt wreaked havoc on my body and I ended up in the hospital. Did I really believe that was how God wanted me to live?

So I worked on me, and with a lot of help from God, I conquered those bad habits . . . I thought.

Years ago, I had given my children into God's care, understanding He loved them more than I did. I thought I had done a great job of letting go and letting God. Then Lorri drove from Salem, Oregon, to Columbus, Georgia.

Oh, I didn't worry about her safety. I knew she was in God's hands.

I didn't worry about the 3,366 miles she had to drive by herself (well, she did have those two cats with her).

I did great *until* she reached Boise, Idaho, and her air conditioner quit working.

It was my helplessness that did me in. I felt it in the pit of my stomach. I could do nothing to help her, and that's when I took it all back—the worry. I drove every mile with her as she sweltered across Wyoming, Colorado, and Texas.

We kept in touch, mostly by texts and Facebook, but when we finally talked I had to confess that her troubles were not just her own. I was being tested . . . and failing miserably.

I flunked again when Lorri's newly repaired air conditioner quit again in Alabama.

Imagine her surprise when the air conditioner began working again when she pulled into her apartment complex parking lot. More proof to me that it was, indeed, my test.

My heart overflowed with gratitude for her safe arrival. I thought my test was over.

Not so.

Two days later, Lorri called and said the car wouldn't start.

Once again, there was that feeling in the pit of my stomach. Did I really not trust God?

I battled for the next two hours, determined to receive at least a D- and not flunk entirely. At first, it was a minute-by-minute handing her back to God. Then I went for five minutes trusting before the fear took over. Finally, I let go completely and placed her back in God's hands.

I trusted again.

Mark 4:40 (NLT)

"Then [Jesus] asked them, 'Why are you afraid? Do you still have no faith?'"

His Door is Open

WHEN I LEAVE THE house, I put Charlie in the backyard. He has very good ears and can hear the garage door open when I return. That's when he dashes to the back door to be let in. However, when the weather grew hot, Charlie discovered a cool spot on the north side of the house. It was by the air conditioner unit and Charlie was no longer able to hear when I come home.

One morning, when I arrived home after doing some errands and grocery shopping, Charlie did not come running to the back door. I opened the door and called his name.

Still no Charlie.

I pushed the door almost shut, but didn't latch it, and then carried the groceries into the house.

Still no Charlie.

I worked around the house a little more, even going to the bedroom on the north side and calling his name. We've taught him how to push a door open, so he could come in if he wanted.

I waited.

Suddenly, there he was at the door with his tail wagging.

"Come on," I called, but he stood there with his tongue hanging out and whole body wiggling.

I thought of some people I know who are standing at the door of a relationship with Jesus. The door is unlatched and ready for them to walk through, and Jesus is saying, "Come on." They stand there being friendly, watching what's going on inside, but never taking that final step of pushing the door open and walking through.

His door is always open.

Luke 14:16-20 (NLT)

"Jesus replied with this story: 'A man prepared a great feast and sent out many invitations. When the banquet was ready, he sent his servant to tell the guests, "Come, the banquet is ready." But they all began making excuses. One said, "I have just bought a field and must inspect it. Please excuse me." Another said, "I have just bought five pairs of oxen, and I want to try them out. Please excuse me." Another said, "I now have a wife, so I can't come."'"

The Balance Beam

MY GIRLS ARE TALENTED in many ways. From childhood, they played one or two different instruments. Practice time was a cacophony of sound. They were also creative, conducting make-believe interviews on the street with friends and family and occasionally strangers. But sports . . . not so much.

Yet, Kerri loved gymnastics. She tried tap dancing and ballet, but when gymnastics time came around, she lit up. And she was good. Her slender body could bend in unbelievable ways. Instead of walking down a sidewalk, Kerri cartwheeled. It looked like she might emerge a real gymnast.

To encourage her involvement, I allowed a strip of masking tape to be placed diagonally across the living room carpet. Balance beams are only four inches wide, but the tape did look a little strange. When visitors came in, it was normal to hear comments like, "Oh, did you tear your carpet?"

Kerri would climb on her imaginary balance beam, and with tongue sticking out, would focus on her balance. Falling off was not acceptable.

She was on her way . . . then came the accident, which ended that specific dream.

While watching the Olympics on television one year, my thoughts returned to that little girl. Kerri not only fell off, but she also never climbed back on. From there, her life went a totally different direction.

Life's like that. Sometimes the path we are on seems even narrower than four inches. We do more than stick our tongue out to help with our focus. In our effort to keep our balance, we may turn to sleeping pills, counselors, Yoga, or just plain whining.

Finding our balance is such a difficult task, but there is one way to keep our focus continually and forever. If we turn to Jesus, the great Balancer, we won't fall off. In fact, when we get to the end of this life, we will land with a triple flip at His feet.

2 Peter 1:5-7 (NIV)
"For this very reason, make every effort to add to your faith, goodness; and to goodness, knowledge; and to knowledge, self-control; and to self-control, perseverance; and to perseverance, godliness; and to godliness, mutual affection; and to mutual affection, love."

Watering a Dead Plant

FALL WAS COMING AND the flowers in pots on the patio looked gangly and used up. It was time to put them away for the winter, except for the lavender. That plant was a perennial, which meant it would bloom again next year. So I transplanted the lavender to the landscaping around the edge of the backyard.

For days it looked dead, lying lifeless on the rocks, but I faithfully watered the limp greenery and faded flowers. Days passed. Then one morning the stems were no longer flat on the ground. Was there life left? Only time would tell.

The next spring, the transplant stood straight, blooms appeared, and it beautified my yard with its lavender flowers.

Recently, with some changes being made in our landscape, that very same type of plant needed to be moved from a corner of the backyard to a spot in front. So I transplanted it, and now it lies on the ground, apparently lifeless. But because I know it can revive, I faithfully water that dead-looking plant every day.

And I wait. Will it spring to life again?

As I contemplated my plant lying on the ground looking lifeless, I thought of how life is like that. When it comes to relationships, sometimes situations change and it looks like that relationship is dead. But if it's important to us, we water it anyway. Maybe it's our relationship with an adult child. It could take years to show signs of life again. Just keep watering.

Or maybe it's a marriage. I've been there. The relationship can revive and become even better than before, but it won't happen by itself. It takes time and effort for me to fill a watering can and walk to the front garden several times a day to water my lifeless greenery, and it takes time and effort to make those wilted relationships come back to life. Just keep watering.

Each year, as we remember the tragedy of 9/11, we can be grateful that even though our nation looked dead and destroyed, we knew we could come to life again. And we keep watering.

Isaiah 60:20-22

"Your days of grieving are over. All your people will live right and well, in permanent possession of the land. They're the green shoot that I planted, planted with my own hands to display my glory. The runt will become a great tribe, the weakling become a strong nation. I am God. At the right time I'll make it happen."

Incongruity

DRIVING DOWN THE STREET, I did a double take. *Is that really what I saw?* I slowed and looked in my rearview mirror. Yes, indeed. A young man dressed in jeans, cowboy boots, and cowboy hat was traveling down the sidewalk on a skateboard.

It didn't seem right. Where was the horse?

I've seen other things like that in my life. For example, the lovely young lady, with fingernails polished, hair styled beautifully, and fashionably dressed—then she opened her mouth. Filth and trash poured forth.

It didn't seem right. Where was the loveliness?

What about marriages? There are couples that seem to have a solid relationship. They attend church every Sunday, their kids are busy with sports and music . . . and one of the spouses is having an affair.

It's not right. What happened to faithfulness?

Incongruity. It's everywhere. I won't even mention politics (although I just did).

Then there are the people who call themselves Christians. They have big smiles on their faces at church, they're ready to help the elderly, available to contribute funds for a project—then comes Monday and a totally different lifestyle. "If that's a Christian I don't want to ever be one," their coworkers whisper to one another. Business owners and professionals say, "I don't ever want them as a customer. They never pay their bills".

And it gets worse. Some Sunday Christians go public with their utter disregard for the message of love we read in the Bible. They blatantly announce things like, "God is a God of hate. He's glad people are being killed in wars."

It's not right. The world should be drawn to Christians because of their love and high principles.

Are my words and behaviors congruent with my professed Christianity? Are yours?

Psalm 101:6

"But I have my eye on salt-of-the-earth people—they're the ones I want working with me; men and women on the straight and narrow—these are the ones I want at my side."

Open Wide

BEING EXAMINED BY AN eye doctor is routine for me. On some visits, my eye pressure is measured; on other visits, my peripheral vision is tested; and other times, pictures are taken that show slices of the inside of my eye. On one appointment for a pressure check, I was told it would take less than 30 minutes.

Not so.

The pressure check, which is a puff of air blown three times into each eye, is always lots of fun. Once that test was completed I should have been right to leave, but the assistant led me to the exam area. The doctor wanted to see me, so I compliantly sat in the eye exam chair.

He walked into the room with small talk and a pat on my knee, then he held down my lower eyelid and put a drop in, moving quickly to the other eye. I expected the sticky, yellow goop the doctor uses so he can see better, but when I blinked, it wasn't sticky . . . and I knew. He had dilated my eyes.

My day was shot.

Driving home would be a struggle because it takes my eyes all day to return to normal after being dilated.

The pupils of my eyes open wide, making it painful to see. I squint, get a headache and a little dizzy, but with the pupils dilated, the doctor can see all around inside my eyes.

Most of us live with the opening into our lives almost shut. Sometimes we allow a few people to see a little more of who we really are. A few of us are braver and allow that opening to grow wider. Our children, spouse, or best friend see some of the ugliness we try to hide. Maybe we're greedy, jealous, judgmental, or full of pride.

Then God comes along. He puts a little drop of conviction in the eye of our heart and our carefully guarded hole opens.

As He examines us, He gives us a record of what He sees in there—it's not pretty. It's painful to see and sometimes ruins more than one day. If we fight against the truth, it can take years, living with spiritual headaches and dizziness, wanting the truth to go away.

If we desire to have clear vision—to be a true follower of Christ—we must allow the Doctor to see all our hidden areas. Only then will we have healthy, twenty-twenty eyesight.

Have you had your eyes dilated lately?

Proverbs 20:27 (NLT)

"The Lord's light penetrates the human spirit, exposing every hidden motive."

The Delicious Center

I HAVE A LOVE/HATE relationship with cinnamon rolls. I love them . . . the flavor . . . the chewing . . . the fragrance. But once they are inside me, I hate what happens to my body . . . my arms . . . legs . . . stomach. So I try to avoid them.

One day, I am sure one jumped onto my plate.

Actually, John and I had taken a little outing to the mall. Of course, I could smell Cinnabon the minute I entered. So we shared one. We cut it right down the middle. That's when I realized I would get only half the delicious center plug—the best part. I always wait until the very end of the roll to eat that delicious last bite.

I used to make pans of cinnamon rolls, but that love/hate relationship didn't work out. I never sit down and just devour the roll. No, each time, I have a plan. I eat around the roll, peeling the sides away—round and round—until all that is left is the soft, cinnamony, frosted center plug. I let the deliciousness roll over me as I slowly chew that ultimate treat.

Isn't following Christ similar? We eat all around the Gospel. We go to Bible studies, sometimes even teach one. We serve in the food line at the Celebrate Recovery meeting, and we never miss a church service. These are all good activities, and we do need to respond if God calls us, but what about that best bite when you know you are right in the center of His will? Everything else falls away and we let the deliciousness of His love wash over us. Best of all, we don't have to cut it down the middle to share. Each of us can have the whole plug. He has enough for everyone.

And you know what? You can enjoy that whole delicious center without any weight gain.

Jude 1:20-21

"But you, dear friends, carefully build yourselves up in this most holy faith by praying in the Holy Spirit, staying right at the center of God's love, keeping your arms open and outstretched, ready for the mercy of our Master, Jesus Christ. This is the unending life, the real life!"

Through the Haze

I HAD TO BE AT work at 7:30, and was headed east, with the rising sun directly in my view through the windshield. And I was able to look straight at it without eye protection. The smoke from fires in our area had caused a thick haze and muted the orb to a pale red-orange. I thought of all the warnings and precautions I've heard about never looking directly at the sun, yet here I was doing it.

I've heard plenty of other warnings and precautions in my many years on this earth. In my earlier days, the warnings were very rigid. "Never go to a movie theater. Those films are of the devil. Never become friends with anyone at school. They are going to hell and might take you with them." And on and on.

So I never looked directly at that sun. I spared my eyes and my life by living in a secluded world.

As an adult, I was given other warnings. After my husband left and we divorced, I was told by pastors and other well-meaning folks that I could never remarry. I must live the rest of my life as a single person. Other warnings included never wearing slacks or attending church without the proper hat and gloves.

I pondered those warnings, but then I re-married, wore slacks, and I no longer own a hat and gloves.

Some warning and precautions are necessary and never change. The Bible gives us guidelines on how to avoid sin. Yet, just as the smoke caused a haze that allowed me to look directly at the sun, life happens—the spouse leaves, the child dies, the money runs out. These experiences cause a haze that blinds the light of the Son. We can look directly at Him and yet not really see His glory. We turn to other things—drugs, alcohol, and in my case, eating. It's a sin to do damage to our bodies, but the pain of living in a broken world can cause the blessings of the Lord to be muted.

So today, even though there are personal fires in my area, I am looking directly at the Son and see Him in all His glory.

1 Corinthians 13:12

"We don't yet see things clearly. We're squinting in a fog, peering through a mist. But it won't be long before the weather clears and the sun shines bright! We'll see it all then, see it all as clearly as God sees us, knowing him directly just as he knows us!"

Interference From the Sun

TELEVISION IS FULL OF worthless stuff. So when I sit down to watch something, I really have a desire to enjoy the whole program. One evening, I was intently focused on a story on TV when the screen went black.

Did I pay my bill? Is the television broken? Thoughts began to fly through my head. I had planned my evening around one program and now it was gone, leaving me highly frustrated. Not sure whether to give up and move on to another project, I waited for something to happen.

And it did. Words appeared on the screen.

We're sorry. We have lost the signal due to interference from the sun. As soon as the interference clears, we will return to your program.

Guess they couldn't fix that.

As I waited, I thought of the times I had made plans and then the Son disrupted them. One such time occurred years ago when I was scheduled for major surgery. I had more than the operation to be anxious about, with three children in need of homes while I was hospitalized. My apprehension heightened when the doctor informed me that my slight fever had caused the surgery to be postponed 24 hours.

I didn't have 24 hours to waste.

So I turned to the Son with my frustrations and concerns. That's when I discovered He had a better plan. As soon as I let go and gave it all to Him, the interference cleared and the surgery could proceed. That 24-hour period was one of the most blessed times in my life.

Have you ever been subjected to interference from the Son?

James 1:2-4

"Consider it a sheer gift, friends, when tests and challenges come at you from all sides. You know that under pressure, your faith-life is forced into the open and shows its true colors. So don't try to get out of anything prematurely. Let it do its work so you become mature and well-developed, not deficient in any way."

Legally Blind

THE DOCTOR'S WORDS ECHOED in my head . . . legally blind. This was my eye we were discussing, not some documentary on television.

For several months I had been aware of failing eyesight. Lying on the bed one day, I realized that I couldn't even see the light fixture in the ceiling with my right eye, although my left eye clearly told me one was there. But legally blind? It sounded ominous.

The doctor didn't stop there. He continued right on with words likes *cataract*, *surgery*, and *twenty-twenty vision*. My blindness wasn't permanent. A cataract is a clouding of the lens that distorts the flow of light and causes dim or blurry vision.

Are you legally blind?

I'm not talking about your physical eye, but your spiritual one. Has your lens grown cloudy with legalism? Has the flow of Light become distorted? God may have given you some specific guidelines for your own spiritual well being. They may or may not apply to someone else.

Don't be legally blind.

How is a cataract removed? The official word is phacoemulsification. This means the cloudy part of the lens is gently washed away. Then a new lens is implanted.

You can see clearly again.

Jesus is in the business of phacoemulsification. His implants always give twenty-twenty vision.

Schedule an appointment right away.

Mark 8:24-24
"He looked up. 'I see men. They look like walking trees.' So Jesus laid hands on his eyes again. The man looked hard and realized that he had recovered perfect sight, saw everything in bright, twenty-twenty focus."

Private Adjustments

As I WALK ON the treadmill at the gym each morning, I can see out the window and down the street. But the gym room is also reflected in the glass. One morning, as I walked and listened to Chuck Swindoll's podcast, minding my own business, there was a sudden movement in the reflection that caught my attention.

By the time I realized what I had seen, it was too late. On a treadmill, two machines over, a young man had decided to adjust his private parts. With his back to the room, he no doubt thought he was safe from anyone seeing him.

How many adjustments do we make as we journey through life?

How many adjustments do we think we've done privately where no one can see? I imagine we would be very surprised to learn how many people have seen those *private* adjustments. They can range from sneaking food (which I've done), keeping some money to yourself and not telling your spouse, right through to having an affair.

We may think we've gotten away with these secretive actions, but there is Someone who knows all about us, every second of the day and every move we make. We have no secrets from Him.

Jeremiah 17:10

"The heart is hopelessly dark and deceitful, a puzzle that no one can figure out. But I, God, search the heart and examine the mind. I get to the heart of the human. I get to the root of things. I treat them as they really are, not as they pretend to be."

Take Off Your Hat

MY DAYS ARE BUSY, so I try to be organized. It seemed like a good plan to go by the driver's license place on my way home from exercise, do some paperwork, pay them some money, and be on my way. I would save time and not have to go back out.

Did I mention I was on my way home from exercise, dressed in sweats and a baseball cap?

Imagine my surprise when they said, "Just step right over here and we'll get your picture taken. You'll need to take off your hat."

No way.

"I'm on my way home from the gym. I didn't realize you were going to take a picture. You really don't want me to take off my hat. Can I just do the paperwork, go home and clean up, and then let you take the picture?"

The answer was no.

And so, for four years, my driver's license has been a constant reminder to me that sometimes efficiency is not all that matters.

That concept is also true in my Christian life. I may have my day planned, with a visit with someone in the middle of the schedule. But what happens when I hear a need behind all the spoken words? Do I say, "You know, I'm not ready for this right now. Can I go home and come back later, when I have my Bible and scripture references ready?"

Or do I take off my baseball cap, and reveal some of my faults and inadequacies? With my flaws showing, they may be more willing to open up.

Sometimes they take off their hat, too.

Luke 18:14b

"If you walk around with your nose in the air, you're going to end up flat on your face, but if you're content to be simply yourself, you will become more than yourself."

Proclamation

I DIDN'T RECEIVE A proclamation from an angel; it was from my mother. When I was 15 years old, the words that came out of her mouth changed my future.

"It's been decided that you will marry the preacher's son."

I said nothing, but my insides clinched. I had questions. *Why? When? Who decided? Don't my wishes count?* But I never voiced them. The why, when, and who were inconsequential. I knew I had no say in the matter. If Mother said it, it would happen.

And it did.

My life was changed forever.

So when I read of an angel appearing to Mary, I have a miniscule understanding of the scenario. Mary may have been 15, maybe younger, when she was told she would give birth. She had questions. She was confused and disturbed. She was unsure if it was true. But she did not remain mute.

Luke 1:34 (NASB)

"Mary said to the angel, 'How can this be, since I am a virgin?'"

After hearing the angel's explanation, Mary graciously submitted, accepting that she would bear a child, even though it was humanly impossible.

And she did. Her life was changed forever.

So in your life, what proclamation have you been given? Did you question it? Were you confused? What was your reaction? Did you acquiesce without a fight? Did you ask for time to think it over? After hearing an explanation, did you understand?

Did it happen?

Was your life changed forever?

Proverbs 3:5

"Trust God from the bottom of your heart; don't try to figure out everything on your own."

Refusing to Trust

Charlie had been given a Christmas present. His tail beat a rhythm against the wall as I helped him unwrap it. Pup-Peroni sticks. He danced around the room as I ripped off the top of the package. Now he could smell it and his enthusiasm grew.

Let me set the stage for what happened next.

Apparently, as I walked on the carpet and rubbed against the Pup-Peroni wrapper, I created an electric charge in my hand. I removed one stick from the package, held it toward Charlie, and he grabbed for it with his mouth. I heard the spark of electricity as he yipped and jumped backward. It had shocked him.

He no longer trusted me.

After that, when I held a treat out for him, he paced the floor and made little growling noises at me. "It's alright Charlie," I'd say, but he didn't believe me. I repeatedly assured him that the treat was his for the taking, with no consequences, but he paced and mumbled.

Humans are just like that. A person we trust burns us, so we refuse to trust again. Perhaps it was an intentional act toward us, or maybe that other person meant no harm. Either way, the result was emotionally painful.

We refuse to trust again.

Just as Charlie missed out on a treat due to his lack of trust, we miss out on many blessings when we protect ourselves. Yes, we may get hurt again, but what about all the treats we miss out on while we pace and mumble about the wrongs that have been done to us?

Do you trust?

Psalm 103:6
"God makes everything come out right; He puts victims back on their feet."

Whose Glasses Are You Wearing?

We had completed an enjoyable time around our table, visiting with friends as we ate dinner. Then John decided to read something to our guests. He walked to the corner of the kitchen counter where he always kept a few of his "cheater" glasses, placed a pair on his nose, and then struggled to read. I watched as he tipped his head one way and then the other.

He couldn't read.

Removing the glasses, he looked carefully at them and then at our friends.

"Did one of you lay some glasses down here?"

Receiving an affirmative answer, he set those glasses aside and reached for another pair on the counter. This time, they were his glasses and he could read.

As I watched that scenario unfold, I thought of how many years I lived my life wearing someone else's glasses. Life was never in focus and was always unsettling. The ideologies that ruled my days never fit what I felt inside. I was wearing someone else's dogma and trying to make it work for me.

Breaking free from lifelong beliefs is not quite as simple as laying down one pair of glasses and picking up another. It requires a sifting of ideas, an analysis of concepts, and being in tune with what you know inside. If you are a Christ-follower, each doctrine needs to be measured against the Word of God. That can't happen in an instant. It took me about two years.

Whose glasses are you wearing?

James 1:5

"If you don't know what you're doing, pray to the Father. He loves to help. You'll get his help, and won't be condescended to when you ask for it."

Priming the Pump

I'VE NEVER ACTUALLY PRIMED a water pump. In books and magazines, I've seen the rustic beauty of a water pump against the backdrop of windswept fields. To operate one, the handle needs to be pumped up and down in order to draw water from underground. Apparently, some take only a few pumps, while others wear you out before the water finally spills forth.

The closest I come to priming a pump is when I replace my Aveeno lotion. It comes in a plastic bottle with a pump on top and I need to prime the pump to draw lotion from a new container.

The same is true when it comes to people. Many times we have to prime the pump to ascertain who they really are. With some people, the information flows quickly and freely. For others, the information is hidden deep within. They may not even be aware of what drives them. Therefore, it takes a lot of priming to get to the real stuff.

As a parent, I learned one way to prime the pump was to take the child for a drive. Something about not having to look in my face gave them freedom to share their dreams, fears, and wrongdoings as we drove the streets.

There is so much value inside every human being. We have to be willing to put forth the effort needed—even if it takes years—to get in touch with the real person.

To prime the pump effectively requires time and a willingness to listen.

James 1:19
"Post this at all the intersections, dear friends: Lead with your ears, follow up with your tongue, and let anger straggle along in the rear."

Perfecting Hypocrisy

MY MOTHER AND I always sat in a front pew at church. We would listen to the preacher on Sunday and testimonies from the congregation (including my mother) on Wednesday. They spoke wonderful, glorious, hallelujah words attesting to their spotless lives. I didn't know about the other people, but I knew my mother's day-to-day life was not like she testified.

With my future husband—the preacher's son—chosen for me, so began my hard-core training in hypocrisy. I was allowed to go to his house on Saturday evenings, but was nervous the first time. I wondered how I was supposed to act. When I entered their home, it seemed the four of us were to gather in the son's upstairs bedroom.

The closet door was opened, a television rolled out and plugged in, and we spent the evening sitting on two beds watching shows like *Gunsmoke* and *Have Gun—Will Travel.* That may not seem like a big deal to you, but on Sunday the sermons were full of "thou shalt nots," and one of those "nots" was watching television. The preacher called it the devil's box and the antenna was the horn.

My training in hypocrisy was in full swing.

When I attended Sunday dinners at their house, my future mother-in-law did most of the talking. She worked her way down the list of everyone in attendance that morning, sharing her thoughts about their clothes, their children, and their mentality. The remarks were ugly. Yet she had smiled that morning as she shook hands with them.

She couldn't stand them, my mother included.

So I learned to wear a mask of hypocrisy. I took my training to heart. I was to be one person at church and a different one the rest of the time. After such powerful training, I had my hypocrisy perfected.

It's hard to believe I used to live like that. Wearing a mask takes a lot of energy. Being real is very freeing.

Do you wear a mask?

Matthew 23:27-28

"Frauds! You're like manicured grave plots, grass clipped and the flowers bright, but six feet down it's all rotting bones and worm-eaten flesh. People look at you and think you're saints, but beneath the skin you're total frauds."

Laundry Day

THE BATHTUB (WE HAD only one) was used for soaking laundry. Since Mother took in washing and ironing, the bathtub had clothes in it quite often, especially whites.

Now she wanted those white clothes to be *really* white, so she added something to the water before placing the clothes in the tub. It was called "bluing," which made fabric appear whiter. But bluing was not permanent and rinsed out over time, returning the clothes to a dingy or yellow cast.

It's the same principle sometimes used by white-haired people, causing them to be called "the blue hairs," but we won't go there.

As I thought about laundry day, I began to compare that process to the journey I've been on in life. The dogma and misguided instructions I received growing up left me with a very dingy concept of life and myself. I put up with it because I didn't know there was a Person who could take care of my dinginess.

Then came the day I placed all my religion and low self-esteem in His bluing to soak. That's when I discovered that His bluing is permanent. It never rinses out.

I'm not saying I don't ever get stains, but with a little soaking in God's Word and some prayer, the stains are removed.

Is it time for laundry day at your house?

Psalm 51:7

"Soak me in your laundry and I'll come out clean, scrub me and I'll have a snow-white life."

The Joy of Blooming

I RECEIVED A BOUQUET of lovely pink tulips one Valentine's Day. I placed them in a vase and sat it in a central location of our home. Each time I looked at them, I felt warm fuzzies. I was loved.

But the progression of their blossoms intrigued me.

The first day or two they stood straight and tall with their bloom closed up. If I stood above them, looking down, I could see the pale yellow center.

The next day, I noticed how they began to bend toward the sun.

As days passed, they no longer stood straight and tall. They leaned a little, allowing me to see the design inside the blossom.

Then they leaned even more and began to droop.

Finally, the petals dropped one at a time.

I am now well into my 70s. I no longer stand straight and tall. (Well, the tall part never happened anyway.) I'm doing some leaning and bending toward the Son. With maturity, I've allowed myself to open up and display the special design I have inside of me.

I've not dropped any petals yet . . . that I know of.

My desire is to give as much joy to others as those flowers gave me. Perhaps the progression of my blossoms will intrigue others to want to know me, to get to know my passions and talents, and to bend with me toward the Son.

1 Peter 3:3-4 (NIV)

"Your beauty should not come from outward adornment, such as elaborate hairstyles and the wearing of gold jewelry or fine clothes. Rather, it should be that of your inner self, the unfading beauty of a gentle and quiet spirit, which is of great worth in God's sight."

Only One Key

THE SKY WAS STILL dark when I drove to the gym. If I didn't get my exercise done then, I wouldn't do it. Years of experience had taught me that.

There was an empty parking space right in front of the gym door. After turning off the car, I gathered the necessary items—keycard to get in the door, bottle of water, paper with my five different routines, headphones, and my iPhone. Then I reached in the zipper pocket on my purse where I kept my car key.

To lock my car, I need the key in hand, then push a black button on the car door handle. The car beeps to let me know it's locked. So I pushed on the black button. Instead of the reassuring beep, a high-pitched whine filled the air. Puzzled, I made sure I had the key in my hand. Sure enough, it was. So I tried again. Another whine.

After three tries, I knew my car lock was broken. Now what to do?

I walked to the front door of the gym where light shone through the glass door. I held the key toward the light to see if there was something wrong with it. Imagine my surprise when it didn't look like my key.

It took a moment for me to realize my error. The night before, John and I had taken my boss's car to the airport so he could drive home after landing. I had placed his spare car key in the zipper pocket on my purse to give to him when I went to work. I had been trying to lock my car with his key.

I traded his key for mine, and it worked.

That happens in life, too. We can repeatedly use the wrong key. Maybe it's a parenting issue. We think if we push harder . . . or longer . . . it will work. But the high-pitched whine continues as we try to make our way through the darkness. It's only when we move to the Light that we can see we're holding the wrong key.

When it comes to life, there's only one Key that works.

2 Peter 2:19-21

"I have a special word of caution for you who are sure that you have it all together yourselves and, because you know God's revealed Word inside and out, feel qualified to guide others through their blind alleys and dark nights and confused emotions to God. While you are guiding others, who is going to guide you?"

Tangled Cords

The young and hip of today use ear buds when they listen to their iPods and iPhones. I am neither, so I use headphones. I keep them in a container in my car along with other items to use when I exercise.

One morning, I stepped on the treadmill and tried to place the headphones on my head, but I couldn't. The cord was too tangled—full of spirals and knots. So I stood with my feet straddled on the edges of the belt while I worked to untangle the cord.

Then this thought hit me: even if I didn't get the cord straightened out, the sound from the podcast would still flow right through the mess and into the headphones.

At times, my life has been a tangled mess like those headphones. I've been sure I could take care of all those spirals and knots by myself. So I worked and worked at it, while the whole time, God was still speaking.

I just wasn't listening.

Proverbs 1:2

"I've called, but you've turned a deaf ear; I've reached out to you, but you've ignored Me."

Wind Gusts and Choices

THE WIND WAS GUSTING up to 40 MPH as I began my drive to Boise. The blasts to the side of my car caused me to hold the steering wheel with a tight grip.

As my hands jerked back and forth, trying to keep the car going in a straight line, I compared myself to a NASCAR driver with a loose racecar.

It would make for a long trip.

After crossing into Oregon and changing freeways, the wind no longer caused issues. In fact, I was being pushed down the highway with the wind at my back.

What a difference that made.

Isn't life just like that? We often feel like we are being blasted on every side, trying to keep a tight grip on what's happening. As we are buffeted, we have choices. Do we keep going the way we are traveling, or do we change direction?

Let God be in charge of the direction. It will make all the difference in the world.

Joshua 24:15 (NIV)
"But if serving the Lord seems undesirable to you, then choose for yourselves this day whom you will serve . . . but as for me and my household, we will serve the Lord."

Leave It

Charlie once attended an eight-week obedience training course. If he passed the ten-point test at the end of the eight weeks, he could be called a "canine good citizen." But to receive that title, Charlie would have to pass all ten items on the test. He could not fail even one point.

The training included commands like "sit" and "stay," but one command was new to me—"leave it." He was tested on his ability to calmly approach another dog. If he lunged or growled, his leash was given a quick jerk and he was commanded to "leave it." At test time, he could show a casual interest in the other dog, but that was all.

Leave it.

Seems like the Bible has some scriptures that give us the same command. When we wrestle with anger toward someone, or have resentment about a wrong done to us, we are told to leave it. Our attention needs to be on God and our blessings instead of reacting to another person or situation. Our goal is to be called a citizen of heaven.

At the end of our life, it's a pass/fail test. Are we willing to "leave it?"

Ephesians 4:31 (NIV)
"Get rid of all bitterness, rage and anger, brawling and slander, along with every form of malice."

Love and Care of Seedlings

RED WAS NOT A Christian, but he was kind of family, married to my brother-in-law's sister. So I had heard all about his misdeeds and been warned about being around him. He smoked and probably drank beer—such a bad sort.

Then came the day he entered the church, walked the aisle to the altar, and asked God to forgive him.

After church, as the faithful churchgoers walked by on their way home, Red stood on the sidewalk and lit up a cigarette.

A lovely old lady saint got in his face and said, "Well, that didn't take long. You've backslidden already."

Similar comments were sent his direction as the word spread about his action. "You're bound for hell with that filthy habit."

Red never came to church again.

That incident came to mind as I worked in my garden this week. We take such good care of little seedlings. We make sure they are watered, and we give them food to help them be healthy and produce wonderful flowers.

Red was a seedling jerked from the ground. No water for him. No kind words. No mention of God's love. He hadn't instantly produced wonderful blooms, so he was cast aside.

I have friends who are seedlings. You probably do, too. Let's make sure they receive the water, food, and love they need. Otherwise, we may never see them blossom.

1 Thessalonians 5:14

"Be patient with each person, attentive to individual needs. And be careful that when you get on each other's nerves you don't snap at each other. Look for the best in each other, and always do your best to bring it out."

Waste is Waste

BACK IN 2013, JOHN and I experienced a four-hour tour of a local area that draws visitors from around the world—the Hanford Site. This area is known for one reason. During WWII, it produced plutonium for America's defense program, including the "fat boy" bomb.

Production ceased in 1989 and the site was left with contaminated buildings, debris, and soil, along with the radioactive reactors. Fifty-one miles of the Columbia River run through this site. Clean up of the waste is vital to the wellbeing of one million people who live downstream (including me).

As we stood on the edge of a giant pit—85 feet deep—our tour guide pointed out trailers that were in the process of being buried. Items of radioactive clothing, pipes, walls, anything that could possibly be contaminated, had been placed in barrels. The barrels had then been placed in the trailers, and the trailers hauled to the bottom of the pit to be covered over.

Then I spied a Waste Management truck traversing downward on the inside wall of the pit. Back and forth it went to a row of Port-a-Potties. When the truck arrived, the driver got out, pulled the hose from the back of the tank, and proceeded to hook it to the first potty.

Waste is waste. Some is radioactive and some is disgusting, but from the worst to the least, it all needs to be dealt with.

Isn't life like that? Some people commit murder, torture, and rape. To our mind, those things are the worst sort of depravity. Families are destroyed and lives changed forever. For the perpetrator, the punishment is severe. They aren't literally buried, but they are placed in confinement, sometimes for the rest of their lives.

But what about bullying? Gossip? Adultery?

Today, more young people are committing suicide due to being bullied. What's the punishment for the bully? Words can destroy a person's life. Affairs destroy families and change lives forever.

There is Someone even better than a Waste Management truck for all these offenses. Waste is waste, and sin is sin.

Mark 7:20-23

"He went on: "It's what comes out of a person that pollutes: obscenities, lusts, thefts, murders, adulteries, greed, depravity, deceptive dealings, carousing, mean looks, slander, arrogance, foolishness—all these are vomit from the heart. There is the source of your pollution."

Project Design

I WAS ORGANIZING MY storage room. One thing I needed was a way to look at my yarns and be able to choose which ones I wanted for my next project. Some yarns are bright, some muted. Others are variegated, which means they can be used with a multitude of different colored yarn. I always try to match the project with the intended receiver, for example:

- NASCAR colors for the afghan I made for the NASCAR fan dying of cancer.
- Green and yellow for the baby born into a family of Oregon Ducks fans.
- For the petite, pregnant young lady, I made a dainty, round afghan.
- Lots of fun colors in the baby afghan for the "hippie" mother-to-be.

Prayers are worked into the yarn as my fingers fly.

Don't you think God is like that? He looks at us, sees us as we really are, and chooses the right circumstances and events to create a pleasing finished project. While He works on us, we are surrounded with prayer and His love as we live each day.

How wonderful that our pattern makes us a unique individual. I'm comfortable in the Master Designer's hands. Are you?

Psalm 139:13 (NIV)

"For you created my inmost being; you knit me together in my mother's womb."

LIFE MOMENTS WITH JOY

Squirrel, Kitty, or Skunk?

IT SEEMED LIKE ANY other normal trip home from work. Driving down a city street, I glanced to my right and saw a man walking on the sidewalk. Suddenly he stopped mid-stride. At that moment, a squirrel emerged from under some bushes and slowly started across the street in front of me.

That's odd. That man must be afraid of squirrels.

That's when I realized the squirrel was black with a white stripe. I froze in mid-drive and slammed on the brakes. At four o'clock in the afternoon, a skunk crossed the street in front of me and calmly walked into the yard of the first house.

If I knew who lived there, I'd call and warn them about who just came to visit. But I'm not walking to that front door.

The man resumed his walk.

I resumed my trip home.

As I drove, I thought how some activities look innocent from a distance. Sometimes, like a child, we may not know the difference between a squirrel and a skunk. As we dabble in the unknown, we may be in danger of being sprayed with a very unpleasant odor.

I know if we observed a child chasing a black and white "kitty," we would immediately reach out to rescue them. What about those around us who are involved in unsavory activities and making unwise choices? Do we caution them? Would they thank us? Or like a child denied its "kitty," would they lash out?

Do we try anyway? Is it our responsibility? Or do we wait for the consequences, the unpleasant odor, to assault our nostrils?

Colossians 3:16

"None of this going off and doing your own thing. Instruct and direct one another using good common sense."

Where's Your Front Porch?

BACK IN THE GOOD ol' days, folks gathered on front porches to discuss everything from weather, to new babies, to politics and religion. Wooden rocking chairs were a staple on the wide sweeping porches, chairs that said "welcome."

Neighbors knew neighbors. Parents watched out for all the children playing in their yard, and kisses for owies or discipline for an infraction were dispensed to all children alike.

By contrast, today's front porches provide a small shelter for the front door. So where is your gathering place now?

Do you remember the old TV show *Cheers*, where people from all walks of life gathered at a bar and everyone knew each other's name? For several years, John and I gathered at a local Starbucks (even though I don't drink coffee). The customers we met there became our "neighborhood." We knew when someone was sick, or moving, or had received a promotion. We celebrated or commiserated together. And we didn't agree on politics.

At church, I am acquainted with people who never fellowship with anyone outside our congregation. Their cocoon keeps them safely inside, surrounded by others who believe the same way. How boring.

For 30 years of my life, I had no friends and didn't know I needed any. It was a stretch for me to reach out to one . . . and then one more. Today, my life is filled with a variety of people of all ages, lifestyles, and philosophies. They know I would drop everything and come running if they needed me, and I know they would do the same.

Where's your front porch?

Proverbs 27:10 (NLT)
"Never abandon a friend—either yours or your father's. When disaster strikes, you won't have to ask your brother for assistance. It's better to go to a neighbor than to a brother who lives far away."

Rescued

THE HOT TUB AT our condo became our gathering place each morning and evening. The rules said only eight people at a time could enjoy it, but sometimes we broke that rule. We met folks from New Zealand, Germany, Japan, and many other places. Their stories were fascinating.

One morning, when the bell tolled eight (opening time), we gathered our towels and headed out. No one else was there. John and I were taking advantage of some couple time when a lady walked through the doorway, turned right, and headed to the swimming pool.

"Oh my goodness. There's a mouse swimming in the pool."

She went into action. There was a "Caution, Slippery When Wet" signboard nearby. She picked it up and put it into the pool. The board had barely touched the water when the mouse scampered up it to the safety of the concrete. From there, it ran into the bushes.

Rescued.

Have you ever felt like you were futilely swimming round and round, and getting nowhere? Your legs are moving as fast as they can, but you're tiring. Soon you will drown.

I've experienced being rescued, both in my life and in my soul. I didn't scamper up the board to escape my robotic existence, but I slowly emerged and became a whole person. My soul was bloody and bruised from false teachings, but there were others who gently lifted me into a right relationship with a loving God.

Rescued.

Ephesians 2:8

"Saving is all his idea, and all his work. All we do is trust him enough to let him do it. It's God's gift from start to finish!"

Misleading Identifiers

I HAD A SMILE on my face as I followed the black Monte Carlo down Clearwater Avenue. Across the back of that car was a sticker . . . "In Memory" with a large red 3. I was driving behind a Dale Earnhardt fan.

My eye doctor's office was ahead on the left. I pulled into the center turn lane, and so did the Monte Carlo. Apparently, the driver was going to the eye doctor too.

I waited until a man climbed from the car.

"I noticed your red 3 and black Monte Carlo. I was a fan of his, too."

"Excuse me?"

"Dale Earnhardt . . . the Intimidator. You're driving a car like his with his number on the back."

"Oh, I don't know anything about that. It was there when I bought the car."

Annoyed, I walked into the doctor's office. *What is he thinking, driving around in a black Monte Carlo with a red 3 on the back if he doesn't even know who Dale Earnhardt was?*

As I waited for the doctor, my thoughts turned to being a Christ-follower.

I've known people who go to church and carry their Bible. Yet, when conversations turned to Jesus, they hemmed and hawed and finally admitted, "I don't really know anything about that. I go to church because my folks/spouse/friend wants me to."

Do I mislead others by my actions or by what I carry? Do you?

2 Corinthians 13:5

"Test yourselves to make sure you are solid in the faith. Don't drift along taking everything for granted. Give yourselves regular checkups. You need firsthand evidence, not mere hearsay, that Jesus Christ is in you. Test it out. If you fail the test, do something about it."

Too Huge to Handle

JOHN AND I WERE exploring the Country Mercantile, a place I had mentioned to him two years earlier. It was only after he visited it with his motorcycle buddy that he deigned it good enough for us to spend time there.

Our plan was to eat some sandwiches for lunch, but first we perused one aisle after another. We were almost to the deli counter when I spied a large glass canister filled with a variety of colored jawbreakers—and not just the normal economy sized ones. These were huge.

I glanced at them again as we passed by. Then, as we waited our turn at the deli, my eyes turned once more to that canister.

"You want one of those, don't you?" John said. "Just go get one."

"Oh, no. They're way too big. I don't think I could even get it in my mouth."

But after another glance, John gave me a little push and said, "Go get one."

So I did.

Once home, I wasn't sure what I was going to do with it. Even though I can open my mouth pretty wide, I couldn't get that huge orb to slide past my teeth. When I put the picture of it on Facebook, a friend suggested I smash it with a hammer.

In my life, I've faced obstacles that seemed too large to surmount. The enormity of my situation had me perplexed and unnerved, but I discovered if I broke that huge problem down—smashing it with the proverbial hammer—I could manage to handle one small piece at a time.

And if I allow God to do the breaking down, it's a cinch.

Ephesians 6:13

"Be prepared. You're up against far more than you can handle on your own. Take all the help you can get, every weapon God has issued, so that when it's all over but the shouting you'll still be on your feet."

One Point

THE NASCAR RACE FOR the Chase was almost over. One more race and the Chase contenders would be decided. Astonishingly, Jeff Gordon, four-time Sprint Cup Champion, was too many points out. This race was his last chance.

He tried and tried harder, but when the checkered flag was waved, Jeff hadn't made it. All because of one point.

He had already driven in 26 races. If he had passed one more car in any one of those races, he would have received that extra point. Or if he had been the driver that led the most laps in a race, that one more point would have been his. Winning a race would have given him three more points.

In the end, he didn't make it into the Chase due to the lack of one point.

Sometimes life is like that. We fall short by one lousy point.

Maybe if we had listened a little longer we would have understood where that other person was coming from.

Maybe if we had stopped our busyness a little sooner, and spent a little more time with our child, the relationship would have gone a different direction.

Maybe if we hadn't ignored our symptoms, the disease would have been discovered in time.

In the end, we don't want to look back and see where we failed because of one lousy point.

Philippians 1:9-10

"So this is my prayer: that your love will flourish and that you will not only love much but well. Learn to love appropriately. You need to use your head and test your feelings so that your love is sincere and intelligent, not sentimental gush."

Turbo or Coasting?

MY CAR HAS A very important letter on it—a T for turbo. When we drove to Banff, Canada, John and I had fun with that turbo. We traveled on mostly two lane roads, in the mountains, with passing lanes few and far between. No matter who was driving, when we needed to pass, we would yell "turbo time" and press on the accelerator. Passing quickly was a cinch. My car is designed for spurts of power.

Some time later, John and I traveled about 30 miles away from home for an evening of fun with another couple. It was 10:30 when we headed home. We passed a sign that said "14 miles to Kennewick."

John glanced at the dashboard where it tells him how many miles of gasoline he has left. Big problem. It showed only six.

Instead of hitting the accelerator, he immediately slowed to below the speed limit. Each time the road had a little downward slope, John put the car in neutral. We glided through the dark, watching the number on the dashboard go from six to five to four to three. It said two when we saw the lights of Kennewick in the distance, and the road was almost all downhill to get there.

We coasted to the nearest filling station.

There are times in life when we need to expend an enormous amount of energy in a brief period of time; we need a turbo boost. When that situation is over, we return to our regular pace of life. Then there are other times when we are low on fuel and need to conserve all the energy we have. We feel like life is passing us by as we cope with an illness or death, but in the distance we can see lights and a re-fueling station.

We can rest in Him . . . the Light of the world. He will supply us with all the power we need, exactly when we need it.

Psalm 23:5b

"You revive my drooping head; my cup brims with blessing."

Simple, but Not Easy

A LOVED ONE WAS nearing the end of his life. I'd been in touch by telephone. I owed so much to him. He helped me find my life. Grief.

Another loved one has had to give up his lifetime passion—music. Who is he without a horn to his lips? Sadness.

Yet another loved one has been given a devastating diagnosis and the future is uncertain. Tears.

I've had a lifelong battle with eye problems, but new symptoms had developed. After three visits to the eye doctor, I'm no closer to resolution. Frustrating.

Then a friend was killed in an accident. Shock.

In all of these situations, I was helpless to change the outcome, but I was in charge of my reactions. I do not have to walk through my days weighed down by sorrow or fear.

I have a choice. It's simple, but not easy.

Each time my mind turns to a sad, tear-producing, frustrating, shocking situation, I remind myself that I've given it to God. I don't have to stress. That's where the hard part comes in. I want to mull over the issue, to fix it, but I leave it with God.

I am living proof that this works. I sleep soundly knowing I'm not in charge.

1 Peter 5:7 (NIV)

"Cast all your anxiety on him because he cares for you."

Just Be

I WAS SITTING IN a hospital waiting room with a friend. She and her husband are good friends and he was having a medical procedure with possible complications. I didn't want her to sit alone.

Turns out she had plenty of family to wait with her, but my thoughts turned to the times I've been the one sitting in some waiting room, with my husband behind those ominous, closed, "No Admittance" doors. At times, I've sat alone. Other times, several friends have waited with me, each person arriving with their own mode of operation.

Some want to talk constantly.

Some seem uncomfortable with the seriousness of the situation, so make jokes.

Others are inclined to go and do something for me or to bring gifts.

Behind all the various behaviors, there is one driving thought. They want to help me through my time of distress.

And then there are those who are just there. No words are necessary. If I have a need, all I have to do is say so. Love and care exude from their presence. They have learned to just be.

As a Christ-follower, my desire is to just be for others. If they want words, I can do that. If laughter would help, that can happen. If a drink from Starbucks would communicate caring to them, I can hop in my car and go.

Above all, I want my love and care to be obvious, as I just be.

1 Peter 3:4

Cultivate inner beauty, the gentle, gracious kind that God delights in."

The Joy of Giving

I LOVE TO GIVE. When I walk the aisles of a store, I'm always on the lookout for something that will exactly suit a family member or friend. My pattern has been to make the purchase and send it on its way, not waiting for a birthday or Christmas. I want them to enjoy it now.

Sometimes I've been disappointed by the receiver. They haven't even bothered to say thanks. More than that, they have not taken care of the gift. Within a matter of days, it is lost or broken. That takes the joy out of giving.

The Bible tells us that God has many gifts for you and me. Do we take the time to say thanks? Or do we take His gifts for granted? When we receive one, do we take care of it? Or do we cast it aside within days, weeks, or months, and then expect more from Him?

I don't want to disappoint Him.

1 Peter 4:10

"Be generous with the different things God gave you, passing them around so all get in on it."

Weeds

EVEN THOUGH THE GROUND may be covered with snow, we know spring is coming. That's when it's time to think about preliminary yard work.

One year, against the scoffing of naysayers, I used a product to prevent weeds. Several people told me it wouldn't work, and my experience with it in the past seemed to confirm their opinion. Yes, I had used it before, but had failed to follow the directions correctly. Therefore, the product had not lived up to its promise.

You see, the product is designed to stop weeds from germinating. If you wait until the weeds exist, it will not kill them. This time, I spread those little granules long before any green poked through the dirt.

This time it worked, just as it stated on the container. My garden beds stayed neat and weed-free all season long.

There is a Product designed to keep our lives weed free, but we need to use as directed. Once that little weed sticks its head up, then it is much harder to control and eliminate. Long before any thistles rear their ugly heads in our lives, we need to daily sprinkle prayer and God's Word all around.

Hebrews 12:15

"Keep a sharp eye out for weeds of bitter discontent. A thistle or two gone to seed can ruin a whole garden in no time."

Stinky Messes

IT'S A REPULSIVE JOB.

As I walked the back yard, eyes searching for the next little present, I thought about what it must be like to have someone available to pick up your messes. Dogs give no thought to the disposal of their excrement. They play, sleep, smell, eat, and poop.

Now before you get too disgusted at my topic and me, hold on. What about us? We go about our daily life—working, playing, sleeping, eating, and making messes, and I'm not talking about the mess left in the kitchen. Who cleans up after us? Sometimes our spouse or friend comes to our aid, but when the fallout of our actions produces consequences for others, where do we turn?

I've had what I consider to be some rather large messes in my life. I'm so grateful I learned about Jesus, who cares about every part of my life—even my stinky messes. He never turns away or holds His nose. He comes alongside and helps me clean up my life, one mess at a time.

Jeremiah 31:23, 25

"A Message from Israel's God-of-the-Angel-Armies . . . I'll refresh tired bodies; I'll restore tired souls."

Scattered Pieces

ONE FRIDAY EVENING, JOHN and I went out to eat with a friend. We'd grown quite close to this young lady, as she stayed with us for about a month, along with her dog, Vivien. During that time, we often left Vivien at home with our Charlie.

Nothing was ever amiss when we returned.

Not so on this particular Friday evening.

After the meal, our friend visited for a while and then went home. I went to our closet to get ready for bed, and what a mess I found. One of John's shoes was still intact; the other had been destroyed and partially eaten.

Who did it? We will never know the answer. Neither dog had an intestinal problem after that night.

Sometimes life is like that. Everything is great; all our shoes are intact and matching. And then life happens. Without warning, we feel like our foundation has been destroyed, with pieces of our life scattered everywhere.

We may or may not know the perpetrator, but that's not the point. It's what you do with those scattered pieces that matters. Life may never look the same as it did before, but you can learn to live with a new normal. The little things, like a friend's touch, mean a lot. Those scattered pieces are not the focus.

Peace, love, joy, caring, and togetherness bring warmth into our lives, and God's love will surround us.

Psalm 51:10

"God, make a fresh start in me, shape a Genesis week from the chaos of my life."

One String

ONE EVENING, THE GREAT Niccolo Paganini was playing one of his favorite violin concertos before a packed house. As he built his performance to its climax, one of the strings broke. With one string dangling down, he never missed a beat. Instead, he improvised with the remaining three strings. And then the unbelievable happened—another string broke. Again, he continued with his concerto on the two remaining strings.

He was almost to the final crescendo of the magnificent concerto when another string broke. The audience watched, spellbound, as he completed his performance on just one string. Paganini spread out his arms and said, "One string and Paganini." Then he bowed.

He made more music out of one string than other violinists do with four.

I have heard of other people who have continued to play with one string. I think of Joni Eareckson Tada, who was paralyzed from the neck down as a teenager. With her one remaining string, she has helped millions of disabled people around the world. I'm sure you can think of others.

My life cannot compare to Joni's, but I have experienced what it is like to continue with just one string. At first, it seemed my remaining string was out of tune and near breaking, but I chose to focus on my one remaining string, rather than on the useless, dangling ones.

And I began to make music again.

You may be staring at your broken strings. They are of no use anymore. It's time to turn to the One String with a lifetime guarantee. Together, you will make magnificent music in your life.

Psalm 92:1-3

"What a beautiful thing, God, to give thanks, to sing an anthem to you, the High God! To announce your love each daybreak, sing your faithful presence all through the night, accompanied by dulcimer and harp, the full-bodied music of strings."

Obsolete

IN 1969, ASTRONAUTS STEPPED on the moon for the first time. In the United States, many people toasted the momentous occasion with Tang. This orange liquid, made from a powder, has also gone to the moon. Its powdered form made it easy to transport in space. Back then, everyone was aware of Tang.

Who talks about Tang today?

In the past, when a team from our church headed off on a mission trip, we would not know of their safe arrival for hours . . . even days. When a team went on a recent trip to Honduras, we all knew of their safe arrival with fifteen minutes of landing, thanks to a post on Facebook.

How many of us write actual letters anymore?

A question in the paper caught my attention. "How long would you last without a mobile phone?" In response to a survey, 47% said they wouldn't last a day. I remember the day, as a child, when we finally got a phone. It was a big deal. Today, thanks to cell phones, more than two in five American adults live in a house without a landline. I haven't had one for years. When will landlines be obsolete?

Our world is changing daily. Items of great importance today will soon no longer matter. As more and more things become obsolete, I'm so grateful I have a timeless God who will still be with me tomorrow and the rest of my days.

He will never become obsolete.

Matthew 28:20 (NLT)
"And be sure of this: I am with you always, even to the end of the age."

It's a Choice

IT TOOK A SEVEN-MILE walk, but I finally made my decision.

Stopping at a pay phone (that certainly dates it), I called my boyfriend and made a statement.

"I've decided to love you."

He didn't think that was very romantic.

Due to my history, I needed to make a very solid choice before I ventured into a serious relationship. Our marriage lasted over 36 years.

It was a choice.

When John developed cancer, I had another decision to make. Did I worry and fret? Or did I trust in the God I said I believed in? No one else can trust for me. So I looked toward heaven and made a statement.

"I've decided to trust You".

He has brought me through so many painful experiences, always by my side. Why should I doubt?

It's a choice.

Hebrews 2:13 (NIV)

"And again, "I will put my trust in him."

A Fine Line

MY HUSBAND STRUGGLED TO take his next breath, which sounded like a grunt. It was not the first grunt.

"John, it's time to go to the ER. You need to be able to breathe better."

"I'll be better tomorrow."

That conversation occurred repeatedly until I used my tough love voice.

"Either you get up and get your pants on, and let me get you in the car, or I'm calling an ambulance."

He put his pants on.

Admitted to the hospital, he was given diuretics to drain the excess fluid from his body, losing twelve pounds in three days. Finally discharged from the hospital, we traveled home accompanied by a prescription for a diuretic at double the normal dose.

Guess what? The medicine worked. Too well.

The above scenario was repeated. He needed to go to the hospital again. This time he was extremely dehydrated. Bags of fluid hung from the IV stand, replacing the water the prescription had removed from his body.

But isn't life like that? Food is good. Too much is not. Too little is not. The same is true in all areas of life. Exercise. Work.

And what about churches? Some churches dole out way too many rules and dogma. Others offer Jesus as a nice guy, but there are other options. Moderation is the key.

It's a fine line.

Colossians 1:23
"You stay grounded and steady in that bond of trust, constantly tuned in to the Message, careful not to be distracted or diverted."

Sorry for Your Loss

I AM A MEMBER of a large church, which explains why John and I didn't know Lisa. We soon learned this wife and mom of three young children had stage-four breast cancer and was not doing well. Our hearts broke for this young woman and her family. My husband had renal cell carcinoma and lung cancer, with a terminal diagnosis, so we were familiar with cancer situations.

For some reason, God had us praying harder for Lisa than we did for John. We shed many tears for their family.

God chose to take Lisa home in 2014. We were so sad for her family, but our grief was not without hope. We knew Lisa was with Jesus and out of constant pain.

Lisa's twin brother Lynn had been one of our pastors. He transitioned to become a family counselor, so we had not seen him for a while.

I made a decision to start the Ideal Protein diet. This required a weekly visit with a counselor, who measures your weight, inches lost (or gained), body mass, etc. At the end of the session, you pick up your "food" for the next week.

As I was leaving my counselor, I noticed a somewhat familiar face. *I know this person, but I can't place him.*

Then it dawned on me. It was Lisa's brother. I hadn't seen Lynn since her death, and he was a mere shadow of his former heavy self. I gave him a big hug and said, "So sorry for your loss."

The look on the counselor's face was priceless.

Lynn had lost 71 pounds and was slim and trim. I could imagine the counselor thinking, *Why would she be sorry about that?* Of course, I had been referring to the loss of his sister, not to his weight, but the counselor didn't know about Lisa.

I knew God had given me a moment of laughter among the pain I still felt for her family.

Ecclesiastes 3:1, 4 (NIV)

"For everything there is a season, and a time for every purpose under heaven, a time to weep and a time to laugh . . ."

No Regrets

WHEN JOHN AND I travelled, I always gave him the top dresser drawer in the motel. He was not very limber and it was easier for me to bend down. I did it willingly.

One day, someone mentioned to me how I had catered to John in the last few years of his life. My answer was quick and sure.

"I know I did, and I'm glad".

I've been in relationships where I had no value. The other person expected me to acquiesce. But in my relationship with John, I gave up nothing of me. I felt good about my decision to honor him.

Now John is gone. I can have whatever drawer I want, and I have no regrets.

I knew my husband's days were numbered, but so are yours and mine. We have no idea when that limb might fall across our house, or if the car coming toward us might change lanes and hit us head on. You could possibly kiss your spouse goodbye in the morning and never see them alive again.

Believe me, when you look at the dead body of your loved one, you don't want to be filled with regrets.

John and I held hands everywhere. A few years ago, a waitress asked if we were newlyweds. John squeezed my hand and smiled at me. "Yes," he said. Every day, we told each other "I love you." Our usual response to each other was: "More." But in his last days, John's response was: "I know."

Just writing that made me cry. It filled me with warm fuzzies to know that he knew.

In the scheme of life, some things aren't worth squabbling over. Live so you can be guilt free and have no regrets.

Proverbs 5:11
"You don't want to end your life full of regrets, nothing but sin and bones."

The Art of Communicating

DUE TO THE MEDICAL history of my family, it is requested that I have a colonoscopy every few years. I know the drill . . . and it isn't fun. When I mention to others I am scheduled for one, the usual comment is: "The worst part is taking the stuff before the procedure."

I agree. It's awful, but it's never been the worst part for me.

After every procedure, John would take time off work because he knew I wouldn't know what I was doing for a day or two. I lived in a confusing, post-anaesthesia fog.

Before every procedure, I would ask the anesthesiologist to please back off on the anesthesia because I have a hard time waking up. They always agreed to do so, placed the IV in my arm, and asked me to count backwards from ten. I could make it to eight before the world went away.

Before my sixth colonoscopy, I knew I needed to speak in a different way to the anesthesiologist. So I told him the stories of past experiences.

I don't take much medicine. One time, when I was hospitalized, they wanted to give me a sleeping pill at bedtime. Though I explained I didn't need it, I was made to take it.

The next day, when I was taken to x-ray, they could not even put me in a wheelchair. I had to be placed on a gurney. I was told later that the radiographer didn't understand why I had been sedated to have an x-ray. It was the sleeping pill the night before.

After several other stories that gave evidence to my susceptibility to sedation, the anesthesiologist said, "I understand what you're telling me. I will start with a little, and then you tell me if you need more."

This time there was no counting backwards.

No feeling of being knocked out.

I could see the screen the doctor was using, and I knew when the procedure had been completed. For the first time, I knew what the doctor told me when it was over. I knew when I went home. I knew what I had to eat. I just *knew*.

No awful feeling.

In our communication with others, are we repeatedly saying the same thing and expecting them to hear something differently? Do we need to tell our story instead of requesting a change in them? Do we understand the art of communicating? It sure made a difference for me.

Acts 15:12-13

"There was dead silence. No one said a word. With the room quiet, Barnabas and Paul reported matter-of-factly on the miracles and wonders God had done among the other nations through their ministry. The silence deepened; you could hear a pin drop."

Whispers

ON A TRIP TO Israel, I was introduced to a technology that was new to me. Our tour guide gave each of us a little power source box to hang around our neck. The box was connected to an earpiece to hang on our ear. That way, we could easily hear her as she explained the various sites we visited.

Sometimes crowds of people surrounded us. Other times, we were alone at an outdoor setting. Even though there was a lot of noise around us, we were still able to hear our guide as she spoke.

The device is called a Whisper.

During my 30-hour trip home, I had plenty of time to ponder. I thought about the Whisper device, and remembered a book I had recently read. It was *The Power of a Whisper* by Bill Hybels. In it, Bill says it takes guts to listen and respond to God's whispers.

But God doesn't give us a device to hang around our neck.

In our busy lives, filled with noise and chaos, we have a choice to make. Do we want to hear God? If so, we have to actively listen. His whispers come in various forms. Sometimes a scripture speaks directly to us. Sometimes His whisper comes through a friend, or the words in a song may suddenly bring new meaning to our heart. A beautiful sunrise or sunset can cause us to pause and listen.

But we have to be aware of those whispers. We have to do more than read words on a page, agree with the friend, listen to the song, view the beauty of the scene, and then go on with our lives without any response.

Our lives will be changed when we listen—truly listen—to His whispers.

Mark 4:9

"Are you listening to this? Really listening?"

Key Not Detected

RECENTLY, I RODE WITH a friend to an out-of-town event, so I left my car key in a container on my kitchen counter. I had a lovely time and returned home Saturday evening.

On Sunday morning, I gathered my purse and Bible, went to the garage, climbed in my car, and pushed the "start" button. Nothing happened. Before my mind had a chance to go through all the possible scenarios, these words appeared on the screen.

Key not detected.

I always carry my key in my purse, and my purse was on the seat beside me. I stared at my purse, puzzled, and then I remembered. My key was still in the kitchen, right where I left it the night before.

Imagine my surprise when I read the title of the sermon on the bulletin: *The Power to Open Heaven for You—we need a key to get in.*

I listened as the pastor explained we would not pass through the door to heaven unless we had a relationship with Jesus. He carries the whole key ring.

Revelation 1:18 (NLT)
"I am the living one. I died, but look—I am alive forever and ever! And I hold the keys of death and the grave."

When I come to the end of my journey here on earth, I do not want to hear "Key not detected."

Matthew 16:19
And that's not all. You will have complete and free access to God's kingdom, keys to open any and every door . . ."

Meet Joy Bach

JOY BACH WAS MARRIED for 35 years to John, a wonderful man who has now graduated from this life's school.

Joy is a mom and grandma who loves to read, write, crochet, knit, sew, travel and go out to lunch. She works as a bookkeeper, but retirement is on the horizon.

Her articles have appeared on the FaithWriters and Jewels of Encouragement websites, and in *Called* magazine.

Over the years, Joy has helped organize and lead singles' groups, taught classes for women, and been instrumental in starting a Celebrate Recovery group at her church.

Joy's newest endeavor is the creation of a group called Reframers. It is for those who may have been given a terminal diagnosis—either for themselves or for a loved one—or experienced divorce or any other unexpected life-altering situation. The goal of Reframers is to laugh each time they meet. Their motto is "Living and loving our new normal."

For more of Joy's articles or to contact her, visit her website at: www.joy-lifemoments.blogspot.com

CPSIA information can be obtained
at www.ICGtesting.com
Printed in the USA
BVHW032241230919
559181BV00002B/227/P